A
DICTIONARY
OF
IGBO NAMES

CHIBUZO N A URUAKPA, PHD

A Dictionary of Igbo Names

ISBN 979-8-6789-0866-7

Printed in the United States of America

To my parents, late Chief Gabriel Amanze Uruakpa (Agụ Ogbuji 1 of Arọ-Ngwa) and Ezinne Rhoda Nkechinyere Uruakpa for their incalculable sacrifice and unfailing love

Without an Igbo name the child has no identity. There is always history behind each name and some of the names speak for themselves.

– Ndiokwere, N. I.

CONTENTS

ABBREVIATIONS

abr int ut	Abridged interrogative utterance
abr ut	Abridged utterance
abr *idiom ut*	Abridged idiomatic utterance
adj phr	Adjectival phrase
adv phr	Adverbial phrase
ax ut	Axiomatic utterance
idiom	Idiomatic utterance
imp ut	Imperative utterance
int ut	Interrogative utterance
med	Medicine
n	Noun
nom phr	Nominal phrase
pos pron	Possessive pronoun
sub ut	Subjunctive utterance (wish)
trad	Traditional
var	Variant

Symbols

( )	Encloses variants in the entry

ABBREVIATIONS

[ ]   Encloses syllables, pronunciation and
        Tones

{ →← } Shows assimilation

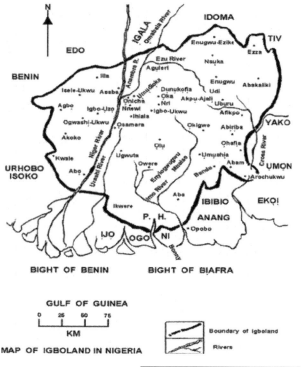

Figure 1 Map of Igboland

Fig. 1, Map of Igboland

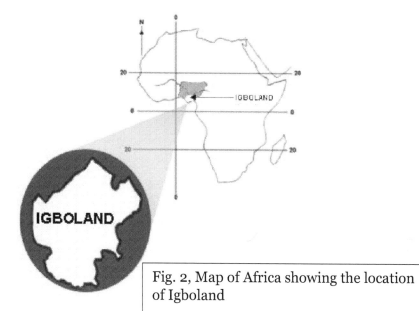

Fig. 2, Map of Africa showing the location of Igboland

Acknowledgements

This book would not have seen the light of day without the invaluable contributions and vital roles played by many people from the formulation of the ideas to the publication of the book.

First and foremost, my wife, the Honorable Judge Vivienne Uruakpa whose love and friendship, moral support and unfailing encouragement fostered a conducive environment and enabling motivation for the long, arduous process of writing this book.

I am indebted to my brother, Barrister Chinwendụ Uruakpa, for his moral support and material contribution to the research phase. Several respondents, too many to mention here, both online, face to face, and telephonically, contributed to the Igbo meanings of many of the names studied in this book. Without their input, this work would not have been a successful enterprise.

I am especially grateful to my daughters, Chiọma and Chiamara, for proof-reading the original

ACKNOWLEDGEMENTS

manuscript and for making very useful suggestions and corrections.

Finally, I wish to express my profound thanks to all my African brothers and sisters in the diaspora, whose umbilical affinity to the mother continent has remained strong and whose peculiar interest in this subject matter and its cultural content served as a significant inspiration for this work.

Preface

The confluence of two incidents led to the writing of this book. The first was the birth of Adanze in 2002. Adanze's parents—Paul and Désirée Benjamin—are family friends from Jamaica and Guyana, respectively. Paul's inquiry about the meaning of Adanze as they were getting ready to welcome their first child was the genesis of this work, as for the first time, I came to realize, on the one hand, this specific need of Africans in the diaspora to reconnect with their roots by giving African names to their children; and, on the other, the woeful dearth of reliable resources to fill this need. Yet, if the seed of this work had been sown, it remained dormant for years, since the work such an undertaking required lay beyond the scope of my research interests at that time.

The second incident took place in the summer of 2013. In a telephone conversation with the service representative of an insurance company, my interlocutor introduced herself to me as what first sounded like "Eugenia". As I repeated the name, she insisted I mispronounced it and spelt it out as U-C-H-E-N-N-A. "Uchenna!" I shouted on the phone while she was still on the second N. "You pronounced it just the way my grandma does," she said in a voice that rang with both surprise and excitement. "That's because I am Igbo just like your grandma," was my answer to her. Before our phone conversation ended, I guided her to properly pronounce her name "for the first time in [her] life" as she gratefully acknowledged.

After this incident, I realized the extremely urgent need to provide an authentic linguistic and cultural resource to be placed at the disposal of people like Paul and Uchenna, and others—including students of Igbo language and culture—who would otherwise have no access to the information contained in this book.

The research phase of this work led me to Ernest Emenyonu's *clarion call* in 1988 for the "[p]reserv[ation of] the Igbo Language for the 21st Century"[1] which heightened my sense of commitment to this all-important enterprise. To fully appreciate the worthwhile nature of both Emenyonu's call and this work, one has to clearly understand the fate of local languages as they struggle to fight off the hegemony and triumphalism of imperialistic languages and cultures that threaten their very existence.

    This existential threat to indigenous languages is made all the more alarming by the ever-widening circles of so-called heritage speakers both within Igboland and in the diaspora who, for pragmatic reasons, use the language with little or no regard for its socio-cultural and anthropocentric foundations and references. In his discourse on what he called "Igbo Experience: A Prolegomenon," Adiele Afigbo expressed a similar concern which is fully cited hereunder:

> […] the claim can no longer be made that all Igbo are born, nurtured and buried in Igbo culture and civilization flowing undisturbed like the river of time. Some are born and nurtured outside Igboland, outside the homeland of Igbo culture and civilization and thus are not authentic carriers of that experience. But what is worse, many of those born in Igboland are born in circumstances which deny them full immersion into Igbo culture and civi-lization. Some are born into families

where Igbo culture is downgraded *vis-à-vis* other cultures, especially Western European culture where English is spoken rather than Igbo and where the overall conduct and comportment of the inmates is Western European rather than Igbo. And for even those born into what may be described as archetypal Igbo families, full access to Igbo culture and civilization is lacking.[2]

Afigbo's example of English language here should be understood as metonymical and representative of all major world languages with potential imperialistic tendencies, and against which Igbo vies for its place in the sun.

It is against this background that Emenyonu's call for *preservation* should be understood and heeded by all Igbo scholars. And it is in response to that call that I have attempted in these pages to provide access to the cultural mines from which Igbo names are dredged up in hopes of thereby contributing, albeit modestly, to the preservation of the Igbo language, culture and civilization not only for the 21st century, but for generations yet unborn.

NOTES

[1] Ernest N. Emenyonu, "Preserving the Igbo Language" in Rems Nna Umeasiegbu, ed., (Enugu, 1988:

   51–63).

[2] Adiele Afigbo. "The Igbo Experience" in Toyin Falola, ed. *Igbo History and Society*, 194.

INTRODUCTION

Spoken by about 30 million people in southeastern Nigeria, Igbo is the mother tongue of diverse people groups who have their homeland in a block of territory delimited to north by the Edo-Igala-Idoma ethnic groups, Urhobo to the west, the Bights of Benin and Biafra to the south and the Ibibio-Anang to the south (see the map of Igboland, fig. 1). These groups who live in the area so delimited are referred to as Igbo and use the Igbo language to communicate their experience of being-in-the-world as well as their overall worldview. Far from being a monolithic society, the Igbo are a mosaic, a conglomerate both linguistically and from the point of view of their settlement. April Gordon writes: "The Igbo are a diverse people of more than 200 groups. Their origins are uncertain, but archeological evidence from the Igbo Ukwu site shows that the Igbo had developed a rich material culture by the ninth century C.E."[1] On his part, Afigbo posits:

The area which they [the Igbo] occupied and whose challenges compelled them to make the adjustments, transitions and inventions which made the evolution of Igbo culture possible is the block of territory defined today by the lower Niger valley, the Nsukka-Udi-Okigwe cuesta and Awka-Orlu uplands, as well as the Cross-River. [...] [T]his is the geographic area bounded than (sic) by Ijo to the south, the Edo to the west, the Igala to the north-west, the Idoma to the north-east, the Ekoid Bantu of the Upper Cross-River and the Ibibio to the east.[2]

From the foregoing, it should be abundantly clear that the term "unity in diversity" aptly describes the more than 200 sub-groups that make up the Igbo ethnic group. And thanks mainly to the onerous and tireless work spearheaded by the Society for Promoting Igbo Language and Culture[3] and sustained by the various Centres and Institutes of Igbo studies in Nigerian universities, and scholarly fora for the advancement of Igbo culture and civilization like the Ahiajoku Lecture series,[4] Igbo language today has attained such a full-fledged linguistic stature that it has little reason to be envious of the so-called imperial languages of Europe.

It should be borne in mind that beyond the territory delimited above, Igbo is also spoken by millions of Igbo who have settled in other parts of Nigeria and many more who have made their homes in other African countries and indeed, other continents around the world. What they all have in common is that wherever they may reside – in Igboland or in the diaspora – they, like the Igbo proverbial tortoise, carry with them their "house," their most easily recognizable cultural identifier, their *Igboness* if you will: their names. These names are the object of our study in the subsequent pages of this book.

* * *

Igbo names are not mere biometric elements or identification labels tagged onto the individual to distinguish them from others; they reflect socio-cultural, philosophical and religious beliefs. They are an expression of long-held societal ethos and often communicate personal life-journeys and life-time family experiences, or even those of the clan. Also, names could reflect parents' aspirations for their children. In other words, names have important meanings and often encapsulate the epistemology and life experiences of their bearers.

Suffice it to say that Igbo names are the most important part of a person's identity as stated in the epigraph. Many of such names, as a result, are full statements of these realities and are therefore long utterances which have had to be shortened. Some examples of shortened names include **Chinua** for *Chi nualu m ogu* (Let God fight for me or the battle is God's), **Ehilegbu** for *Ehi l'egbu (or Ubochi ana-egbu) onye-efu, ka m ghara ino n'ulo* (The day an innocent person is killed or persecuted, may I not be around, meaning God forbid that I take part in killing (persecuting) an innocent person), and this writer's last name – **Uruakpa**, which is the short form for *Uru akpaghi onye nwere aku* (A wealthy man is never dishonored or held in derision,) among many others.

It must be pointed out, at this juncture, that given the vast diversity of the Igbo, there are variants in the spelling of the same name, depending on the dialect. A typical example is the name **Ihuoma**

4

(common in Aba-Owerri-Ụmụahịa-Ọkigwe area); in Ọnicha-Nnewi area the same name is *Iruọma*, while in Abịrịba-Arochukwu-Ọhafịa area, it is *Ivuọma*. As much as possible, I have strived in this book to provide these variants in the orthography of the names, for the various dialects all contribute to the richness of the Igbo we speak today. At the same time, I must confess that not all dialects are covered in this seminal work and those covered have not been identified by name.

NAMING CEREMONY

Traditionally, names were given on the eighth day, which coincided with the traditional circumcision rituals for male children (Uchendu, 59). The naming ceremony thus assumed a religious dimension as the child was given a name the same day of his mystical union with the land of his birth since his blood from the circumcision would make contact with the ground, thus signifying, perhaps, in a most symbolical fashion, the child's double affinity: to the clan and to mother earth.

All male children were circumcised on the eighth day (Uchendu, 50), except in the case of families that had experienced recurring infant mortality. Such parents could elect to leave their baby boys uncircumcised for fear of their dying in the process of circumcision. The uncircumcised boy would still be given his name on the eighth day, and would later be circumcised during his pre-adolescent years, usually between the age of ten and twelve. Any male who grew up into adulthood without being circumcised was not considered a full-fledged man or member of society until he was circumcised. Thus, belated—adolescent or adult—circumcision was a grand ceremony, the social significance of which was like finally assuming one's place in society.

Unlike male circumcision, which was done on the eighth day, excision when it was carried out for girls, was made to coincide with the period of *Mgbede* usually during late adolescence. As Uchendu points out, "In southern Igbo communities, a girl waits until maturity before her clitoridectomy[5] which takes place during her *Mgbede* (fattening seclusion of an adolescent girl)" (59). He adds: "This fattening seclusion was quite common though not always followed by clitoridectomy, in many other Igbo communities" (59). As a social function, the child's naming ceremony is a festive event attended not only by the extended family, but is open to everyone in the community. "Receiving a name is an impor-tant event in a child's life for he is socially accepted as soon as he is given a name. The "name-giving" ceremony, a formal occasion celebrated by feasting and drinking, is also an occasion which generally articulates the different social groups to which the child belongs." (Uchendu, 60).

Who Gives the Names?

As is the case in many African societies, it is the role of the Igbo father to give his child his or her name. While he may confer with his wife and the extended family, the name chosen for the child will be pronounced for the first time during the ceremony by the father, or the mother (in the father's absence.) However, the birth of a child might have different significance to different people, much as each person might have different aspirations for the same child. In other words, the parents might each have a different name for their child, in which case the name given by the father will be the child's first name, while that given by the mother becomes the middle name. More often than not, the grandparents also have their own names for their grandchild, as well. In that case, this child might have up to four names, or even more.

When a child is believed to be the reincarnation of a relative—parents, grand-parents or even great-grandparents—the first name of the reincarnated relative could be given to the child. Sometimes, the parents could choose not to give the child this name, but a name that suggests this reincarnation: **Nnanna** (Grandfather), **Nnenne** (Grand-mother) or **Nnealọ** (also **Nneayọ**) (Mother has returned), etc. In the olden days, reincarnation wasn't just assumed (even if there were some clear signs: close resemblance, some physical body marks, etc.), but was ascertained by a seer, the priest or priestess of a deity, who would consult the oracle and spirit world of the ancestors to authenticate the suspected reincarnation. Only then was there validity in naming the child after the reincarnated relative.

It is important to point out at this juncture, that reincarnation in traditional Igbo religion could be referred to as a process of 'redemption,' a process that affords the reincarnated person the opportunity to seek to make amends for their life's errors, a sort of personal atonement in order to attain *ancestorhood*. According to Enyeribe Onuoha, "In Igbo cosmology, the end of man's life is the attainment of ancestorhood. To qualify for this, a man would have purged himself of all serious imperfections through several reincarnations."[6] In other words, reincarnation in Igbo traditional religion is a teleological phenomenon that has its sights squarely set on ancestorhood.

Every Igbo name thus has a lot to say about its bearer as a person, or their family or clan. Conclusively, names in Igboland have socio-cultural *meanings* and are deeply rooted in the cultural worldviews and mores of the people.

INSPIRATION FOR AND SOURCES OF NAMES

Igbo names have several provenances and are deeply rooted in real-life experiences of the parents, family history and projection into the future in the form of parents' aspirations for their children. Parents have recourse to a variety of names and the ones they choose for their children depend to a large extent on what they want to convey through their children's names to the larger society, and to the world. A survey of Igbo names reveals the following categories.

1. Didactic and Moral Instruction

Some names have didactic significance, meaning that they are intended to teach certain moral lessons and convey societal ethos inherent in the Igbo cultural heritage. Such names include ***Anyaegbulam***, ***Eme-zuo***, ***Nwakaego*** and ***Ọnụbụọgụ***, among others.

2. **To Foster Family and Clan Mythology**

Names like *Alaǫma*, *Alaukwu*, *Amadiegwu* and *Ụlǫakụ* are given as a way of fostering family or clan mythology. Through these names, parents are able to express their patriotic and family pride.

3. **Aspiration to Greatness**

Some names reveal the parents' aspirations to greatness which get projected onto their children. In other words, such names indicate what the parents want their children to become when they grow up. Some of such names include *Adaeze*, *Akajiakụ*, *Ezeji*, *Nwanyịeze*, among others.

4. **Praise of God's Attributes**

The very high frequency of Igbo names prefixed or suffixed by *Chi* or *Chukwu* demonstrates the centrality of God in Igbo cultural worldview and conveys the various attributes they ascribe to Him. "Most Igbo names, Ndukaihe points out, [...] opine the place of God in their belief system. They show how

God is always present and share (sic) in the daily struggles and vicissitudes of human existence" (224). Some of these names include **Jaachike, Chiagba-nwe, Eberechukwu, Izuchukwu**, among many others.

5. Existential Vulnerability

The names **Adịele, Amaefule, Anyatọnwụ** and **Ejitụ**, each conveys the angst of existential uncertainty and vulnerability. Through them, parents are able to articulate their philosophical stance in the face of life's great challenges.

6. Identification With and Dedication to Deity

See the Religious Dimensions of Igbo Names below for the dedication of children to deity in Igboland in names such as **Anyanwụ, Nwosu, Nwanị, Nwamụọ** and **Nwagwụ**.

7. Celebration of Nature

Some Igbo names are given to convey specific attributes and characteristics of creatures and phenomena that exist in nature. From the majestic rivers and towering trees to fierce mammals, these names are given to conjure up specific imageries and attributes. They include **Anyịm**, **Nwagụ**, **Ọdụmegwu**, **Osisioma**, and many more.

8. Days of the Igbo Week

Some names are given to mark the day of the week on which their bearers were born. The Igbo week is eight days made up of two sets of four market days: one set the major and the other the minor market days. The major market days receive the suffix *ukwu* and the minor ones the suffix *nta*. The market days are *Eke, Orie, Afọ* and *Nkwọ* in that order. Each week thus has an *Eke-ukwu* followed by the other three market days in the *-ukwu* series; and an *Eke-nta* followed by the other three market days in the *–nta* series. From one *Eke-ukwu* or *Eke-nta* to another is thus eight days, which make up the Igbo week. Names which indicate the day of one's birth include **Ekenma**, **Nwafọ**, **Nwaorie**, **Okonkwọ**, among others.

9. Igbo Ethics and Morality

There are names that convey Igbo society's standards on moral duty, principles and practice. These names encapsulate what the Igbo as a people see as morally acceptable or reprehensible. Among such names are **Ajụnwa**, **Ajụrụ**, **Akụdo**, **Ebekunwanne** and **Ehilegbu**.

10. Reincarnation

As stated in the preceding section, some names indicate the reincarnation of departed family members. An important type of reincarnation is the notion of the spirit-child, *ọgbanje*,[7] who chooses a cyclical reincarnation. An *ọgbanje* does not live long, but dies suddenly and mysteriously in infancy or during the teenage years; and is believed to reincarnate again and again, until the spirit of *ọgbanje* has been appeased. It is only after a successful appeasement that the cycle of reincarnation of the *ọgbanje* is broken. Some of these names that invoke reincarnation include **Nnanna**, **Nnealọ**, **Nnenne**, **Nwaọbịa**, among others.

RELIGIOUS DIMENSION OF NAMES

The Igbo are a deeply religious people[8] as can be seen in the names they give their children. The epithet 'religious' should be understood not in the narrow sense of the Judeo-Christian acceptance of the word, but in the broader sense that the Igbo believe that all human actions and experiences, all natural phenomena, and indeed the entire cosmos, all lead to an ultimate reality, ordered and controlled by a transcendent being. As is evident from the preceding section, Igbo names reflect this worldview.

In the olden days, some children were dedicated from birth, sometimes from conception, to the service of a deity—a god or goddess—and this was reflected in the name given to them. **Anyanwụ** was the name given to a male child dedicated to the sun god. **Kanụ**, **Kalụ** or **Kamalụ** to a male child dedicated to the god of thunder. Some of these names have continued to the present, but have shed the religious dimensions and practices associated with them, others have gone out of use as the religious rituals and exigencies are no longer practised. A girl named **Nwanyịagwụ** (Priestess of a deity), for instance, was fully devoted to the service of the deity and never got married. If she ever got married, it would be to a priest of the same deity, who would offer the prescribed sacrifice to redeem her from her devotion to the deity. This explains the reason behind the name **Chievo** (the gods have saddled me with a heavy responsibility).

Traditional Igbo society believed in and practised polytheism. There was a god of thunder, god of harvest, the sun god, river god, god of war, etc. The most prominent divinity was **Ala** or **Anị**, the earth goddess, who "became the main object of worship throughout Igboland" (Afigbo, 198). Her counterpart, **Chukwu**, the sky god, according to Afigbo, hardly received any worship (ibid) even though he was considered the greatest among these divinities having created the earth and everything in it. He was thus also known as **Chineke**, the god of creation. Maybe his "splendid isolation" (Afigbo, ibid) in the sky, in other words his remoteness, explains why he received little worship from the Igbo, while each clan and kindred had a shrine for *Ala*. Agbasiere observes that "[a]lmost every Igbo village has a shrine (which is distinct from the shrine of any local divinity referred to as *ihu agbara*), which is called *ihu Ala*" (Agbasiere, 52).

In addition to these gods, there was the personal deity **chi**, the providential god, who was more like a guardian spirit that attended to each person.[9] Referring to **chi** as a "spark of God's creative force," Enyeribe Onuoha explains **chi**'s function as accompanying "each human being as his mentor or guardian angel throughout life. Before each soul begins its earthly sojourn, it first enters into a solemn pact with its CHI, a contract sanctioned by God and later imprinted on the palms of both hands—as AKARA-AKA mapping out the course it is to follow in life" (Rems Nna Umeasiegbu, 84). The Igbo believe that since the world is so vast, complex and mysterious, mortal knowledge alone is inadequate to successfully navigate through its maze of systems. Each person thus requires the assistance of a **chi** who knows the humanly unknowable and can see what no mortal eyes are capable of seeing, for there are mysterious worlds, beings and realities far beyond and distinct from the physical world. The reality of these mysterious and often hostile forces makes it imperative that humans be surrounded by powerful allies with superior intelligence, perfect knowledge of, and supernatural power over, our universe in order to counteract the powers and influences of these adversaries.

This traditional religious philosophy was to find its confirmation and fuller expression with the advent of Christianity. The evolution from polytheism to monotheistic Christianity, however, was not automatic as many societies held tenaciously onto their traditional practices. But they found the commonality of a supreme God who created everything reassuring. And if the Igbo reluctantly let go of their gods and goddesses as they embraced Christianity, their concept of a personal god made this new religion both *ancient* and *modern*. This is to be seen in the many Igbo names that have either **Chi** or **Chukwu** as a prefix or suffix. For this personal God has become one and the same as the Supreme God of the Bible, whose attributes are as varied as He is infinite, and as the language could give expression.

THE IGBO PHONETIC SYSTEM

The Igbo Alphabet

In this book I have adopted with modification the New Standard Orthography (NSO) used by Echeruo (x). The two modifications to the NSO have to do with the following:

i) restoration of the subscript dots to the closed vowels i, o and u as used in the Official Orthography of 1961 also known as the Ọnwụ Orthography in which they are written thus: ị, ọ and ụ; and

ii) restoration in the alphabet of the diagraph 'ch' for the voiceless palato-alveolar affricate for which Echeruo used the monograph 'c'. While it is true as he pointed out that: "Nowhere in the Igbo language does a situation arise in which "**ch**" is in complementary distribution with "**c**"" (xi), it is rare in common practice to find any name with the voiceless palato-alveolar affricate 'ch' written with a '**c**' as Echeruo systematically did for both common and proper nouns in his book. Yet, not even Echeruo himself could implement the switch from the diagraph 'ch' to the monograph 'c' he eruditely espoused, as far as names are concerned.

For instance, even though Echeruo wrote the title of Pita Nwanna's novel as *Omenükö* from the original orthography *Omenụkọ*, he maintained the Official Orthography's use of the diagraph 'ch' in the names Chinua Achebe and Chukwuemeka Ike within the same paragraph (Echeruo, x).

Moreover, the author wrote his name as **Echeruo** throughout his book, pointing out that "[s]pelling usages for personal and place names [...] have remained largely unstandardized, and [his] dictionary has not attempted to impose a method of re-writing these names" (Echeruo, xiv). As a result, for clarity and in order to maintain the familiar integrity of Igbo names, I have used the diagraph 'ch' throughout this book.

The Igbo alphabet used in this book is as follows:

a, b, ch, d, e, f, g, gb, gh, gw, h, i, ị, j, k, kp, kw, l, m, n, ṅ, nw, ny, o, ọ, p, r, s, sh, t, u, ụ, v, w, y, z.

PRONUNCIATION OF LETTERS OF THE IGBO ALPHABET

Vowels

There are eight vowel sounds in the Igbo vowel system, each of which is a long sound. These are:

a [aah] as in ca**r**d
    aba (bottle, branch), **aka** (hand), **atọ** (three), **aziza** (broom)

e [éé] think of doubling the [e] sound in **e**ight
    eju (snail), **eku** (wooden spoon), **ede** (cocoyam) **eze** (king, tooth)

i [ee] as in the word **ee**l

ise (five), **isi** (head, smell, blindness), **igwe** (heaven, steel)

ị [i] as in **i**ll

ịta (chew), ịnwụ (to die), ọchị (laughter), gị (you, *sing.*)

o [oh] as in **o**de

oche (chair), **iso** (to follow), **obodo** (land, country, nation)

ọ [or] as in **awe**

ọma (good), **afọ** (belly, stomach) ọzọ (again, monkey)

u [oo] as in z**oo**

uche (thought, opinion), **idu** (to lead), **unu** (you, *pl.*)

ụ [ʊ] as in f**oo**t

ụzọ (way or road), ụfọdụ (some), **azụ** (fish, back or behind)

Consonants

There are 28 consonants in the Igbo alphabet, each of which is pronounced with an i [ee] sound, thus:

b bi [bee]   **bịa** (come), **ebube** (glory), **aba** (bottle)

ch chi [chee]   **chi** (god *or* goddess), **echi** (tomorrow), **nchefu** (forgetfulness)

d di [dee]   **daa** (to fall), **ide** (to write), **idu** (to lead)

f fi [fee]   **ife** (to fly), **ifufe** (wind), **ifu** (to get lost)

g gi [guee]   **gị** (you, *singular*), **ige** (to listen), **ịgụ** (to read, count)

gb gbi [gbee]   **egbe** (gun, hawk), **igbanwe** (to change), **igbu** (to kill)

gh ghi [ghee]   **ụgha** (a lie), **aghụghọ** (trick, sly), **ighe** (to fry)

gw gwi [gwee]   **igwu** (to dig), **ọgwụ** (medicine, pill), **ugwu** (hill, north)

h hi [hee]   **aha** (name), **ehi** (cow), **ahịa** (market)

j ji [gee] **aja** (sand, sacrifice), **ije** (walk, journey), **jide** (to hold)

k ki [kee] **aka** (hand, handle), **karịa** (very much), **ụkọ** (want, need)

kp kpi [kpih] **mkpa** (need), **ikpe** (judgment), **ịkpa** (to weave)

kw kwi [kwih] **ikwe** (to agree, believe), **okwu** (word, speech)

l li [lee] **lee** (look), **ili** (to bury), **ilọ** (to return)

m mi [mih] **ịma** (to know), **mụọ** (spirit), **imi** (nose)

n ni [nih] **nụrụ** (hear, *imper*), **unu** (you, *plur*), **ọnọdụ** (position)

ṅ ṅi [ŋih] **aṅụ** (bee), **ịṅụ** (to drink), **ọṅụ** (joy), **aṅụrị** (happiness)

nw nwi [nwih] **nwa** (child), **anwụ** (sun), **inwe** (to have), **ịnwụ** (to die)

ny nyi [nyih] **anya** (eye), **enyi** (friend), **onyinye** (gift)

p pi [pih] **puta** (come out), **opi** (horn, flute), **puku** (thousand)

r ri [rhi] **aro** *or* **nro** (dream), **iri** (ten), **ura** (sleep)

s si [sih] **ise** (five), **isi** (head), **site** (from), **osisi** (tree)

sh shi [shih] **ishi** (head), **ishi** (blindness), **shie anya** (be bold or daring, Echeruo, (150))

t ti [tee] **taa** (today), **ato** (three), **teta** (wake up)

v vi [vee] **ivo** (to weed), **mvo** (nail), **vuru** (to carry)

w wi [wee] **were** (to take), **iwe** (anger), **uwe** (shirt, clothing)

y yi [yee] **iyi** (stream), **oyi** (cold), **oyiyi** (resemblance)

z zi [zee] **azu** (fish), **iza** (to answer), **ozo** (again), **aziza** (broom)

The reader will notice that although Igbo names could begin with all eight vowels (even though 'ị' occurs in the initial position in only two names), only 12 consonants are found in the initial position in Igbo names, including 's' and 't' which begin only one and two names respectively.

It is also important to point out, at this juncture, that some consonants – b, d and g – are sometimes realized with aspiration in some words. This aspiration is indicated in this book with /bʰ/, /dʰ/ and /gʰ/ respectively when it occurs in names.

Diagraphs

Of the 28 letters of the Igbo alphabet, 9 are diagraphs.[10] In addition to **ch** which occurs in English words—**ch**air, wret**ch**ed, cou**ch**—though not as a diagraph, there are these other diagraphs **gb**, **gh**, **gw**, **kp**, **kw**, **nw**, **ny**, and **sh**. These diagraphs should not be treated as consonant clusters as Igbo language is not characterized by this phonetic phenomenon found in Indo-European languages.

Since there are no consonant clusters in Igbo, when two consonants follow each other, they are treated as diagraphs of a single sound and are realized in one articulation. The realization and articulation of these sounds are peculiar to the *Kwa* group of languages and do not, with the exception of **ch**, **kw** and **sh**, directly correspond to English sounds. The following are the realization and articulation of these diagraphs and some tips for their pronunciation.

ch is a voiceless palato-alveolar affricate that approximates the English /tʃ/

> **ch**eta (remember), e**ch**i**ch**e (thought), ọkọ**ch**ị (dry season)

gb is a velarized bilabial implosive and the pronunciation is realized with one voice emission and not as a cluster of two different consonant sounds:

> **gb**uo (to kill), ị**gb**anwe (to change),
> nso**gb**u (difficulty, problem).

gh This voiced velar fricative approximates the aspiration produced in the articulation of the interjection of disgust 'ugh':

> a**gh**a (war), a**gh**ụ**gh**ọ (trick, slyness),
> nche**gh**arị (repentance, change of mind).

gw The articulation of the consonant cluster in the name Gwen will help speakers of English to produce the voiced labialized plosive in Igbo words:

agwa (measles), igwe (heaven, steel),

egwu (dance, wonderful).

kp is a voiceless velarized bilabial implosive, the key to the production of which is the term *implosive*. Instead of the English plosive /p/ which is produced with aspiration of air from the lips, the Igbo /kp/ draws air into the velar section of the mouth.

akpa (bag), mkpate (stirring, whipping

up), ikpere (knee).

kw This voiceless bilabial velar plosive is produced through the same articulation as the English sound for /qu/ as in question, quest, and inquiry. Examples are:

akwa (egg, cloth, cry), ekwe (wooden

drum), ikwe (mortar, to believe).

nw The voiced labialized velar nasal is produced by nasalizing the voiced labialized velar sound in whine or wine. Examples include:

nwa (child), ọnwa (month or moon),

ọnwụ (death).

sh This voiceless palato-alveolar fricative is articulated exactly the same way in Igbo as in English /ʃ/ as in shall, should, Irish. Examples:

ashi (a lie), ishi (also: isi (head)), oshi

ọnwụ (a dare-devil).

The Prominence of the Vowel / Syllable

As previously stated, Igbo is a member of the *Kwa* family of African languages[11] and is characterized by the pronunciation of each of the syllables in any given word, the foundation of which is the vowel. Because each vowel is given prominence in pronunciation, no two vowels can belong to the same syllable, except in the case of proper nouns, in which the same vowels following each other could get assimilated into each other. For instance, in the name **Chibụzọ**, there is assimilation – a sort of syneresis of the two [ụ] sounds (Chi bụ ụzọ) (*God is the way*) → (Chi b{ụ→←ụ}zọ) → Chibụzọ [chí-bū-zò]. This is what Emenanjọ calls "complete assimilation" (Emenanjọ, 22–23).

There is also "conditional assimilation", according to Emenanjọ (ibid). Consider Chi bu ụzọ (God comes / is first) (Chi-bu-u-zọ) [chí-bù-ù-zò].

29

Because the two vowels in presence are not the same sound (u and ụ), there can be no assimilation, unless "the speed of the utterance is rapid" (ibid, 23), and therefore each of the vowels must belong to different syllables. This non-assimilation coupled with the resulting change in tone makes for clarity in meaning and distinction between the two utterances Chibụzọ and Chi bu uzọ.

In a nutshell, the Igbo lexicon shows a concatenation of consonants and vowels and while a vowel could form a syllable of its own, no consonant can constitute a syllable on its own with the exception of syllabic nasals. Also, no two consonants can belong to the same syllable, unless the consonants are a diagraph. Note that unlike the Indo-European languages, Igbo has no double consonants, except for syllabic nasals.

The Syllabic Nasal

One major phonetic phenomenon that characterizes the Igbo language and that is central in our study of Igbo names is the syllabic nasal. Through this concept, *m* and *n* function as vowels by forming their own syllable when they are followed by specific consonants. Emenanjọ (xxii) sets forth the following syllabic nasal principles:

"m before the labial sounds p, b, m, f, v, kp, gb and before the semi-vowels w and y;

n before other consonant sounds"

Examples of syllabic nasals with 'm': **mpi** [m-pì] (horn), **mbụ** [m-bú] (first), **mma** [m-mà] (knife), **mfepụ** [m-fé-pù] (flight), **mvọ** [m-vó] (fingernail), **mkpa** [m-kpà] **scissors**, **mgbakọ** [m-gbá-kò] (gathering), **mweda** [m-wé-dà] (lowering, humility), **myọ** [m-yò] (sieve).

Examples of syllabic nasals with 'n': **ndidi** [n-dì-dì] (patience or endurance), **njikọ** [n-jì-kó] (link(s), tie(s) or bond(s), **nkume** [n-kú-mè] (rock or stone), **nleda** [n-lé-dà] (contempt, disrespect), **nna** [n-nà] (father), **nrọ** [n-ró] (dream), **nsogbu** [n-sō-gbú] (disturbance, problem or trouble), **ntụte** [n-tú-té] revival, **nzọpụta** [n-zó-pù-tá] deliverance.

Please note that these syllabic nasals are not pronounced as [em] or [en], but roughly as [mm] for both.

The Voiced Velar Nasal

In addition to the diagraphs and the syllabic nasals, another important phonetic concept relevant to our study of Igbo names is the voiced velar nasal (ṅ). This letter represents the same sound represented in the International Phonetic Alphabet (IPA) by /ŋ/, and found in English words like singing, song and bring. Examples are **aṅụ** (bee), **iṅụ** (to drink), **ṅụrịa** (rejoice) and **ọṅụ** (joy).

IGBO TONAL SYSTEM

Igbo is a bi-tonal—high-tone, low-tone—language. Both Emenanjọ and Echeruo identify and apply these two tones. "Igbo is a 2-tone (High, Low) language", writes Echeruo (xiv). "Igbo has two distinctive tonemes, High, which is unmarked, and Low, marked `, as well as the tonal phenomenon known as the downstep" (Emenanjọ, 11). While I have followed these categories, I have gone a step further, for clarity of pronunciation and meaning, in providing marking for these distinct tones and the downstep "tonal phenomenon" thus:

> High tone marked [']
>
> Low tone marked [`]
>
> Downstep tone marked [¯]

Clarity in pronunciation and meaning demands that the tones be indicated in order to enhance the semantic distinction of lexical items, since a change in tone leads to a change in meaning. A word like *isi*, for instance, could have any of four different references depending on the changes in tone, thus:

> í-sí (head)
>
> í-sì (smell)
>
> ì-sì (blindness)
>
> í-sī (to cook)

In order to eliminate all ambiguity, I have tone-marked all the names provided in this book. Occurring in isolation, and devoid of any context, proper nouns would easily lend themselves to gross mispronunciation if they are not fully marked, especially so for non-native users. As a result, I have avoided the use of H and L in square brackets after a word to indicate high and low tones as adopted by Echeruo. The full tone-marking I have shown in this work is, however, not without any technical difficulties with regard to the orthography of the names, as the subscript dots cannot be applied to letters that are tone-marked. This means that for names in which subscript dots appear, I have had to sacrifice the dots (in the guideline for the pronunciation of each name) in order to provide the appropriate distinctive tones. For instance, in the entry for the name **Achọlọnụ**, while the subscript dots are indicated in the name, only the tones are provided in the section aimed at aiding in the pronunciation of the name: [à-chó-ló-nū]. As a result, non-Igbophone users will find it extremely useful to first familiarize themselves with the pronunciation of the subscript-dotted-vowels, in particular, and the letters of the Igbo alphabet in general, before attempting the pronunciation of the names in this book.

THE EVOLUTION OF THE ORTHOGRAPHY OF IGBO NAMES

The Igbo that is spoken and written today has gone through a series of sustained evolution process to get to its current state. From the contemptible assessment given of it in 1884 by a British Colonial Official, Reverend Metcalfe Sunter, Igbo has steadily evolved from a language that could interest only "the comparative philologist and never likely to become of any practical use to civilization,"[12] to its current status as the vehicle for one of the major West African sub-regional cultures and one of the most prevalent and easily recognizable African languages in the diaspora.

Missionaries were the first to transcribe Igbo language into written form, before 1929 when R. F. G. Adams and Ida Ward introduced phonetic symbols to represent Igbo sounds for the first time (Oraka, 96). This was the beginning of what came to be referred to as the Ida Ward Orthography. From these initial baby steps, the Igbo language would reach a groundbreaking stage with the formal launching of the Society for Promoting Igbo Language and Culture at Denis Memorial Grammar School in 1950 as a "national cultural association" (Oraka, 95).

This body will go on to play a pivotal role in standardizing Igbo orthography, grammar and lexicon, and in promoting Igbo cultural education and scholarship. One of the major contributions was the introduction of "the use of diacritic marks to distinguish the 'light' and 'heavy' vowel sounds and O, U and U (sic) as at present" (Oraka, 97) as the Ọnwụ Orthography Committee of 1961 accepted the recommendations of the S. P. I. L. C.

These decisive steps toward standardization contributed to raising increasing awareness among Igbo elites whose pride in Igbo language and culture reached a level never seen before in the 1970s. The socio-cultural climate of the post-civil war years was optimal for the 'cultural revolution' of the 70s as the Igbo were recovering from the devastating effects of the Nigerian civil war.

When Igbo names were first written in Roman (European) orthography they were written in such a way as to make them pronounceable by the British. Igbo itself as a word was written as *Ibo* or *Iḅo* for a very long time for the simple reason that the British found it difficult to articulate the velarized bilabial implosive sound /gb/. Igbo words and names with [a] and [e] final sounds were written with an **h** while words with the ọ-sound were written with **or** to aid in their pronunciation. But with the introduction of the diacritic marks proposed by the Ọnwụ Orthography Committee, names like **Obiomah** were now written as **Obiọma**, **Nkumeh** as **Nkume**, **Ezeh** as **Eze**, and **Ezenwah** as **Ezenwa**. Similarly, from then, **Kanayor** or **Anayor** was written as **Kanayọ** or **Anayọ**, **Offor** or **Ofor** as **Ọfọ**, **Chibuzor** as **Chibụzọ**, and **Iheanachor** as **Iheanachọ**, etc.

The cultural revolution mentioned above was especially given greater impetus as prominent Igbo leaders took decisive steps to assert and promote their *Igboness*. Sir Francis Ibiam, first Igbo governor of the Eastern Region during the First Republic, honorary Knight Commander of the British Empire, KBE (1951) and Knight Commander of the Order of St. Michael and St. George, KCMG (1962), for instance, had "returned his knighthood and renounced his English name, Francis, in protest against the British government's support of the Nigerian federal government"[13] during the civil war. Until his death in

1995, this great Igbo leader was officially known as Dr. Akanụ Ibịam and by his traditional titles: Eze Ogo Isiala 1 of Ụnwana (Afikpo) and Osuji of Uburu.

This unprecedented, courageous cultural revolt set the stage for the Igbo to boldly embrace their Igbo names and reject the Western names they had been given at baptism or when they enrolled in schools. For instance, the civilian administrator of East Central State was officially known as Ụkpabị Asịka throughout his stay in office. Nobody knew him by his Western first name, Anthony.

This cultural reawakening also meant that Igbo names were now increasingly being written the Igbo way especially so, following the standardization efforts of the Society for Promoting Igbo Language and Culture. Nevertheless, since it was impossible to uniformly implement the recommendations of the Standardization Committee across the Igbo citizenry, these recommendations have had to exist side by side with the old forms, including the orthography. In other words, while the standard language is used in formal circumstances: from primary school to institutions of higher learning, in print and electronic media, in government and academic scholarship, etc.;

there are no means of enforcement of the standardization at personal and interpersonal levels. As a result, no uniformity exists in the way people write their names.

Consequently, in this book, I have provided not only the various dialectal forms of the names as stated earlier, but also their various orthographic forms. An example is the name ***Echewaọzọ*** for which there is the dialectal variant ***Echewaọdọ***, and each having an orthographic variant: ***Echewaozor*** and ***Echewa-odor*** respectively.

HOW TO USE THIS BOOK

For native speakers who also read Igbo, this dictionary is very easy to use as each entry has an English translation and a pronunciation guide with tone-marks. In addition to these, for the interest of non-native speakers, many entries have commentaries that place them squarely within their cultural contexts. A few names whose English meanings are obvious to all speakers of English are not followed by cultural comments. Each name is written in its proper Igbo orthography, including subscript dots and superscript dots where they apply. And where applicable, variants of the names— dialectal or orthographic—are provided in parentheses together with the grammatical category of each name. Enclosed in square brackets following each name is the guide to its pronunciation including the applicable phonetic tones.

The dictionary is divided into two parts for boys' names and girls' names, respectively. While some names are gender specific, a good number of Igbo names are used for both genders. The user will find the entries for such unisex names in both parts of the dictionary.

Finally, let me reiterate an earlier appeal to non-native users of this dictionary: at the first blush, Igbo names could look intimidating. But their pronunciation is very highly phonetic and systematic, and the key to unlocking it is provided in the Orthography and Phonetics sections of this Introduction. The user-friendly information presented in that section is provided as a tool to help non-native users achieve near-native pronunciation of Igbo names, and with confidence. When that happens, the objective of this introduction will have been achieved.

NOTES

[1] April A. Gordon. *Nigeria's Diverse Peoples*, 36.

[2] Adiele Afigbo, "Igbo Experience: A Prolegomenon" in Toyin Falola (ed.), 187.

[3] See the excellent article written by L. Nnamdi Oraka, "The Role of F. C. Ogbalu," 94–106.

[4] See Raphael Chijioke Njoku, "Imperial History," 48–49.

[5] Uchendu defines *clitoridectomy* as "Female circumcision involving the excision of the clitoris" (59).

[6] Enyeribe Onuoha, "The African Traditional World View," 91.

[7] According to A. C. Agwu, "It is believed that the spirit of such person hover (sic) around river banks, thick forests and sometimes in the wilderness where they (the spirits of young people) wait to enter the womb of women to be reborn. They are referred to as 'Ogbanje' or 'Ogbaburu Onaje'," 7.

[8] "Religion, according to Gloria Chukukere, is not just "something" that a person accepts on growing up, but is as part of his physique as the air that he breathes," 15.

[9] Gloria Chukukere, 15.

[10] The phonological description of diagraphs are adapted from the Emenanjo's *Elements of Modern Igbo Grammar*, 9–11.

[11] Citing the linguistic works of R.G. Armstrong, C. Wrigley and R. S. Smith, Afigbo writes: "Igbo is one of the languages which linguistis (sic) designated *kwa*, a sub-group of the Niger-Congo group of languages. Other members of the *kwa* in our area include the Yoruba, Edo and Idoma. On the basis of glotto-chronological evidence, scholars have come to the conclusion that languages in the *kwa* sub-group must have started diverging, that is assuming their distinctive and individual forms, at least 6000 years ago" (Afigbo, 169). The list of Kwa languages should include Fon and Asante (see also Elizabeth Isichei, 155.

[12] Cited by L. Nnamdi Oraka, 96.

[13] https://en.wikipedia.org/wiki/Akanu_Ibiam (Retrieved July 20, 2018).

PART ONE

BOYS' NAMES

A

Abalefu *int ut* [à-bʰ á-lé-fū] Who would dare to issue an unfounded, frivolous rebuke or threat? This name also means: "Could an idle or empty hand lead to riches?" In that case the voiced bilabial will be pronounced with no aspiration, thus: [à-bá-lé-fū].

Abangwu *nom phr* [à-bá-n-gwù] The bough or branch of a "large prominent hardwood tree that serves as an ancestral landmark" (Echeruo, 107). See *Ọjị* or *Osisịọma* for other names relating to trees.

Abaraonye *int ut* [à-bʲ á-rá-ó-nyé]
Who has the audacity of raising these
intimidating rebukes or threats? Some
parents see the occasion of naming a
child as an opportunity to respond to
their detractors, adversaries and
opponents. *Abaraonye* is one of such
names through which parents can
respond.

Achilefu *int ut* [à-chì-lé-fū]   Who
would laugh for no reason? Meaning:
there is always a good reason why
someone will start laughing.

Acholonu *ut* [à-chó-ló-nū]   Words
of mouth not backed up by action are
inadequate in any meaningful pursuit.

Adiele *imp ut* [á-dí-ē-lé]   Let's keep
watching (hoping). In other words, let's

keep our fingers crossed. With little or no advanced neonatal care, many children died before their first birthday. Some families experienced higher incidence of infant mortality than others. As a result, the joy that greeted the birth of a child was tempered by the apprehension that s / he might not live long. The name *Adiele* is thus the cautious admonition of 'let's wait and see' or 'let's not rejoice yet.' It might also apply to other situations of uncertainty in the family. For instance, if an elderly member of the family is seriously ill and their recovery is doubtful, a child born to this family at this time might be named *Adiele*.

Adimuko *ut* [á-dìm-ù-kó]   I am unique or priceless. See the entry for this name in the Girls' Names section.

Everything said about the girl's worth equally applies to the boy who bears this name.

Agbanwe *adj phr* [á-gbá-nwē] Constant, never changing. Short form of *Chiagbanweghị* (God never changes).

Agha *n* [á-ghá]   War. This is one of the names given to mark a significant event (given to a boy born during the war). It could also be used figuratively to refer to a war going on in the lives of the parents.

Agụ *n* [á-gū]   Tiger. This emblematic name for majesty and power is given to boys in a society in which bravery and prowess are the indices of masculinity.

Agubeama *abr ut* [á-gú-bé-á-mā] When the lion roars in the street, we know who the brave men are.

Aguiyi *n* [á-gú-í-yī] Crocodile.

Aguwamba *abr ut* [á-gú-wá-m-bā] Each people or nation has its own warrior(s). The full name is *Aguwa mba, agunye dike*: (if you take stock of a people, you must come across (a) warrior(s)).

Ahamba *nom phr* [á-hā-m-bā] The name, fame or reputation of a people, town, clan or even race.

Ahuchogu *abr ut* [á-hú-chá-á-ò-gù] Warrior only at home. In other words, after cowardly avoiding fights outside, when at the home the person terrorizes everybody.

Ahụrụonye *int ut* [à-hù-rù-ò-nyé] This rhetorical question from an all-conquering hero is literally asking: "Whom did I see?" that is, "who could stand up to me?" or "who was brave enough to challenge me?" The needless answer implicit in this taunting question is: *no-one.* This name celebrates victory in war, wrestling or other traditional sports. It is also the self-congratulatory, chest-beating cry of the person who roundly defeats his opponent(s).

Ajụnwa *int ut* [à-jú-nwá]   Can one reject or abandon one's child? Child abandonment is one of the **nsọ-ala** or **nsọ-anị** (abominations) that anyone could ever commit. Children are a

49

spiritual link to the ancestors and as a result, there is a mystical, supernatural bond between them and the spirit world. And anyone who mistreats them, let alone, abandon them will face the wrath of **ala** or **anị**, the earth goddess. *Ajụnwa* is therefore a rhetorical question that is informed by this belief, the logical answer to which is a resounding *no*.

Ajụrụ *abr int ut* [à-jù-rù]   Were due consultations made? In a society where decisions are made based on due process of consultations and deliberations, the question uppermost in everyone's mind before verdicts are reached is always whether all avenues have been exhausted. Parents could give their child this name in order to draw attention to botched proceedings or irregularities thereof.

Akachi *nom phr* [á-ká-chī], (*var*: **Akachukwu** [á-ká-chū-kwū]) God's hand. This name given to boys and girls alike, celebrates God's protection in the parents' lives and his protection in their families' experiences. In other words, the name *Akachi* really refers to the protective hand of God. It evokes God's hand as a shield that creates safety and security for the family in the midst of existential dangers.

Akadike *nom phr* [á-ká-dí-kē] Warrior's or great man's hand(s) or arm(s); (understand: strength or power).

Akajiakụ *nom phr* [á-ká-jī-àkù]
Literally: the hand that holds riches;
meaning a prosperous person.

Akalefu *int ut* [à-kà-lé-fū]   Who
would complain for no good reason?

Akataobi *adv phr* [à-ká-tá-ó-bī]
When one forebears or endures the load
is light. This name speaks to the capacity
to persevere in the face of untold
hardship, intense provocation or even
great danger. Endurance is one of the
virtues inculcated into young boys
through traditional sports such as
wrestling, and through initiation rites
into age-group societies in which boys
are prepared and equipped to face life's
challenges as they grow into manhood.

Akọ (*var*: **Akor**) *n* [à-kó]   Ingenuity.
Akọ refers to slyness, cleverness, that creative genius in the individual that makes him not only unique and original, but above all, able to analyze complex situations and issues with ease and come up with appropriate solutions.

Akọma *abr ut*   [á-káá-ó-mā]   With determination and fortitude, no challenge is insurmountable.

Akpamgbọ *nom phr*   [à-kpà-m-gbọ] A bag of ammunition.   An unusual name, this military epithet is given to boys to convey a sense of invincibility and preparedness for any situation.

Akụbụike *ut* [à-kù-bú-í-ké]   Wealth is empowering.

Akụchie *adv phr* [à-kù-chi-é] When wealth is plentiful or in abundance. It is a common belief among the Igbo that riches do not last forever, they are seasonal, transient and must be harnessed and protected, otherwise, they easily dry up; and when that happens, the consequences are disastrous. As a result, when the source of wealth is still flowing is the time to harness and invest it before it dries up.

Akụdo *nom phr* [à-kú-ú-dō] Wealth gotten by honest means. Traditionally, the Igbo were mainly farmers, traders and crafts persons, and held the belief that ill-gotten wealth was an abomination. An honest poor person of integrity was honored and respected in society, and any person whose wealth came from dishonest means was ostracized by the community. *Akụdo* is an open and public declaration that one's livelihood streams down from the lofty hills of integrity and honesty. It is also an implied charge to the baby boy who bears it to pursue and uphold a life anchored in honesty.

Akụneto *abr ut* [à-kù-ná-ē-tó]   As wealth increases, so does the number of those who enjoy consuming it.

Akwaelumọ *ut* [á-kwá-é-lū-n-mó-ō], (*var*: **Akwaerumụọ** [á-kwá-é-rū-n-mó-ō]   Weeping does not move the spirits, deity or the ancestors.

Alaọma *nom phr* [à-là-ó-má]   Good land, meaning good village, town or city. This name is normally given to a child whose parents either settled away from home or got married outside their kindred. The name is a tribute to, and a grateful acknowledgement of, the hosts' hospitality. *Alaọma* could also refer to one's own city or town, in which case it is speaks of the parents' patriotic pride.

Alaukwu *nom phr*   [à-là-ú-kwú] Great land. Like *Alaọma* above, *Alaukwu* is a patriotic statement of pride in one's land, city, town or clan. The greatness of the land, of course, derives from that of the inhabitants and therefore, *Alaukwu* is not-so-veiled a reference to one's aspirations to greatness.

Alọzie *abr ut*   [á-lọ-zí-é]   When one is born into the right family, the prospect of achieving one's destiny is assured. Being born into the right family means one is on right side of Providence, and therefore, has a future that will unfold exactly as it has been laid out by Providence. This existential reassurance is the very thrust of the name *Alọzie*. This name could also refers to the idea of being reincarnated into the right family.

Ama(h) *n* [á-má] *Ama* refers to family, household or clan. The name celebrates the family unit as indivisible and central to the life of the community. It also speaks to the Igbo philosophy that places communal life above the individual, the nucleus of which is the family.

Amadị *n* [à-má-dí] A great man or noble man. The pursuit of greatness is at the heart of industry and hard-work which characterize the Igbo. In traditional society, greatness was achieved in agriculture, commerce, sports, artisanal craftsmanship and war. Today, the same pursuit is the motivating factor behind their distinguished accomplishments in all fields of human endeavor and both within the country and in the diaspora. It is still an honor to be called *Amadị* or *Nwamadị* (the son/daughter of a great/noble man).

Amadịegwu *nom ut* [á-má-dī-é-gwù] Wonderful or awesome family, household or clan.

Amaechi *abr ut* [á-má-é-chī], (*var:* **Amechi** [á-mé-chī]) The family (under-stand: lineage or clan) will not end as long as there is a [male] child.

Nothing is more haunting or devastating to the Igbo existential psyche than the thought of one's (family) name not perpetuating itself. This fear fed the propensity of many men to marry a second, third or even fourth wife. It was common for a man who has had all daughters or no child at all to marry again in quest of a male child to keep the family name alive. It was not uncommon in those days for the first daughter of the family to have a male child at her parents' home before getting married in order maintain the family name. In that case, her male child belonged to her parents and not to her or her husband, if and when she eventually got married.

Amaefule *sub ut* [á-má-é-fū-lē] (*var*: **Amaefula** [á-má-é-fū-lā]) May the family or clan endure. *Amaefule* is normally given to a child, boy or girl, born into a family that has experienced series of tragic events. It is thus a prayer that the family be spared any further occurrence of tragedy so there could be posterity.

Amaka *abr ut* [à-má-ká]   A child who is the epitome of beauty. The name can also be pronounced [á-má-kā], in which case it means family is supreme. *Amaka* could also be the short form of *Chiamaka*, God is infinitely good.

Amakọlam *imp ut*   [á-má-á-kō] May I never lack a family, household or clan.

Amala *n* [á-má-à-là] Native-born. A member of the community or clan who enjoys full rights and privileges thereto appertaining.

Amanze *nom phr* [á-má-n-zē] The family or household of chiefs or noblemen.

Amauche *int ut* [à-mà-ú-chē], (also: **Amauchechi** [à-mà-ú-chē-chí] Does anyone know God's mind or plan ?

Amobi *abr ut* [á-mō-bì], (*var*: **Onyeamaobi** [ò-nyé-á-mā-ó-bì]) No one knows the heart.

Amụta *abr ut* [á-mú-tá] After a child is born, the heart is settled.

Anele *imp ut* [á-ná-ē-lé], (*var*: **Anene** [á-ná-ē-né] Let's keep watching (hoping). This name is a variant of

Adiele above. See Adiele for the full context of this name.

Aniẹkwe *abr ut* [à-nì-é-kwē], (*var:* Alaekwe [à-là-é-kwē] The land (goddess) forbid (that I go childless, for instance). The land goddess **Anị** or **Ala** was a benevolent goddess who acted as an ally to the citizens, especially those who walked uprightly, and whose 'hands were clean.' **Anị** would not allow any evil to befall such people. *Aniẹkwe* is thus a thankful acknowledgement of her protection.

Anọruo *abr ut* [á-nō-rú-ó] Time to settle down. This name is given to the male child of a man or woman who has a hard time settling down at home. The name literally means now that he or she has a child, may he or she see reason to settle down.

Anozie *abr ut* [á-nō-zí-é]   When one occupies one's rightful position in the family destiny is sure to be fulfilled.

Anubiri *imp ut* [á-nú-bī-rí]   I/We have heard enough. Parents who are childless or have only daughters always have an earful: gossips, theories, unsolicited counselling, diagnoses and medical recommendations, etc. When the parents finally have a child, they issue what could be referred to as a "cease and desist" appeal to all and sundry by naming their child *Anubiri*.

Aṅubiri *imp ut* [á-ṅú-bī-rí]   Let all the gloating and rejoicing stop. The message of this name is addressed to foes and opponents who gloat over the childlessness or lack of a male child in the family.

Anya *n* [á-nyá]   The eye(s).

Anyadike *nom phr*   [á-nyá-dí-kē] The eyes of a great or brave man stare down and intimidate all opposition.

Anyaegbulam *sub ut* [á-nyá-é-gbū-lām], (*var:* **Anyaegbunam** [á-nyá-é-gbū-nām])   May my eyes not covet to my hurt. The Igbo consider covetousness immoral and they call a covetous person '*Onye anya ukwu*' (a person with big eyes.) *Anyaegbulam* is a wishful prayer that one be preserved from a covetous disposition.

64

Anyahụrụ *nom phr* [á-nyá-hù-rù] Eyes that have seen it all.

Anyanwụ *n* [á-nyá-nwū] The sun. This name was given to a male child dedicated to the sun deity.

Anyaọha *nom phr* [á-nyá-ò-hà], (*var:* **Anyaọra** [á-nyá-ò-rà] The cynosure of all eyes. The eyes of every member of the community. This name also means the eye that sees for all.

Anyatọnwụ *abr idiom ut* [á-nyā-tá-ó-nwū], (*var:* **Echetọnwụ** [é-chè-tá-ó-nwū] When one remembers death. The Igbo regard death as the sole mitigating factor against man's capacity to plan and execute. In other words, without death, man would be invincible, and only death stops him in his tracks toward the realization of his full potential. As a result, when one remembers death, there is some sort of existential stock-taking that takes place.

Anyịm *n* [à-ny-ì-m]   River. Also tortoise. The latter is regarded in Igbo mythology as the most cunning and sly of all the animals, as it survives against all odds and is able to wriggle out unscathed of any dangerous situation.

Arịnze *abr idiom ut* [à-rí-n-zè]   But for God's grace, things would have been worse.

Asịegbu *abr idiom ut* [á-sī-é-gbū], (*var:* **Ashịegbu** [á-shī-é-gbū]) Contempt (though disturbing and annoying) is not deadly.

Asịka *abr idiom ut* [à-sí-kā] Lying is worse than a enmity.

Asonye *inter ut* [à-só-nyé] Whom do I avoid? Or whom do I trust? As this name implies, the parents who give this name to their son see themselves as surrounded by opponents and enemies, and do not know whom to trust.

Atụlaegwu *imp ut* [á-tū-lā-é-gwū] Do not be afraid or fear not.

Awuzie *abr ut* [à-wú-zí-é] Arrival into wealth. Full name is *Awuziera akụ*.

Azịkiwe *idiom* [á-zī-kī-wé] Children are more prone to tantrums and blowups.

Azụbuike *idiom* [à-zú-bú-í-ké]
Posterity is strength.

Azụka *idiom* [à-zú-kā] Posterity is greater.

CH

Chesarachi *imp ut* [chè-sá-rá-chī]
Commit your concerns onto God.

Cheta *imp ut* [chè-tá] Remember.

Chetachi *imp ut* [chè-tá-chī], (also:
Chetachukwu [chè-tá-chú-kwú])
Remember God.

Chetanna *imp ut* [chè-tá-n-nà]
Remember your father.

Chetanne *imp ut* [chè-tá-n-nē]
Remember your mother.

Chiagbanweghị *ut* [chí-á-gbā-nwè-ghì] God never changes.

Chiagọzie *ut* [chí-ā-gō-zī-ē] God has blessed.

Chiavọghị(lefu) *abr ut* [chí-á-vò-ghì(-lé-fù)] Each day dawns with its own challenges.

Chibudo *ut* [chí-bū-ū-ɗó] God is peace.

Chibụeze *ut* [chí-bū-é-zè] God is king.

Chibụihe *ut* [chí-bū-ì-hè]   God is light. Also means
God is the source of all enlightenment.

Chibụike *ut* [chí-bū-í-ké]   To God belongs power.

Chibụgwu *ut* [chí-bū-ù-gwù]   To God belongs honor.

Chibụnna *ut* [chí-bū-n-nà]   God is a father.

Chibụọgwụ *ut* [chí-bū-ó-gwū]   God is healing; literally: God is medicine.

Chibụzọ *ut* [chí-bū-ūzō] God is first, meaning   God   is   pre-eminent. Pronounced this way, *Chibụzọ* literally means *God comes first*. When it is pronounced as [chí-bù-zō], it means God is the way.

Chidera *abr ut* [chí-dé-rà-á]   Once God has decreed or ordained anything, it is final. The Igbo believe that one's destiny is written on the palm on his / her hand by God; and this destiny is immutable. Chidera literally means that once God has written anything (understand: destiny), it is permanently unalterable.

Chidi *abr ut* [chí-dī], (also: **Chukwudị** [chú-kwú-dī])   God is; meaning: God exists or there is God. This is a name given by parents who have been through great ordeals and survived against all odds. *Chidị* is a testimony of divine intervention without which life wouldn't be possible. A declaration of God's goodness in the parents' lives, *Chidị* is also the short form of other longer names derived from it, as in the next six entries. In those instances, *Chidị* means *God is*, and is completed by whatever attribute of God that follows it.

Chidịebere *ut* [chí-dī-è-bé-rē̄] God is merciful.

Chidịndụ *ut* [chí-dī-n-dʼù] God is alive.

Chidịnma *ut* [chí-dī-n-má] God is good.

Chidike *ut* [chí-dī-í-ké] God is powerful / great.

Chidiẹbube *ut* [chí-dī-è-bù-bè]
God is glorious.

Chidịnso *ut* [chí-dī-n-sō] God is
ever near.

Chidịnsọ *ut* [chí-dī-n-só] God is
holy.

Chidozie *sub ut* [chí-dɔ̄-zí-é] May
God preserve.

Chiebuka *ut* [chí-ē-bū-ká] God is
the greatest.

Chiechefulam *sub ut* [chí-é-chē-fù-
làm] May God never
forget me.

Chiedozie *ut* [chí-é-dɔ̄ ó-zí-é] God
has pre-planned and preserved.

73

Chiemela *ut* [chí-ē-mē-ē-lā]   Thanks be to God or God has done marvelously.

Chiemezuo *ut* [chí-é-mé-zū-ó], (*var:* **Chiemezue** [chí-é-mé- ū-zé])   God has fulfilled His promise.

Chievo *abr ut* [chí-é-vō]   God or the gods have saddled me with a great responsibility.

Chigbolụmọgụ *sub ut* [chí-gbō-ó-lúm-ò-gù], (*var:* **Chigboọgụ** [chí-gbō-ó-ò-gù] or **Chigbo** [chí-gbō-ó])   May God intervene in my struggles; also may God mediate my conflicts.

Chigbundụ *abr ut* [chí-gbú-n-ɗù]
If God spares my life.

Chigozie *sub ut* [chí-gō-zí-é]   May God bless.

Chigoziri(m) *ut* [chí-gò-zì-rì(m)]   (I am) blessed by God.

Chijioke *ut* [chí-jī-ō-kē]   My share is with God.

Chika *ut* [chí-kā] (*var*: **Chukwuka** [chú-kwú-kā])   God is supreme. This name is also the short form of longer names as shown hereunder.

Chikadibia *ut* [chí-kā-dí-bī-à]   God surpasses or is greater than doctors.

Chikairo *ut* [chí-kā-í-ró]   (*var*: **Chukwukairo** [chú-kwú-ká-í-ró]) God is greater than the adversary or the enemy.

Chikanma *ut* [chí-kā-n-má]　God is supremely good.

Chikere *ut* [chí-kē-rē] Created by God.

Chikerendụ *ut* [chí-kē-rē-n-dⁱ ù] God is the creator of life.

Chikereụba *ut* [chí-kē-rē-ù-bá], (*var:* **Chikerụba** [chí-kē-rù-bá] or **Chikelụba** *ut* [chí-kē-lù-bá]) Wealth is from God.

Chikezie *abr ut* [chí-kē-zí-é] Whatever God has made or created is perfect and cannot be improved upon.

Chikwem *abr ut* [chí-kwém]　If God permits me or God being on my side. As much as the Igbo believe strongly in industry and hard-work, they also believe in destiny and providence. In other words, hard work alone does not guarantee success in life. They strongly believe that for a person to be successful, God has to crown his or her efforts and industry with success. Many a hardworking person is known to struggle to make ends meet, and *Chikwe(m)* is an indirect appeal to God for leniency and mercy based on this philosophy.

Chikwendu *abr ut* [chí-kwé-n-dʰū] If God grants life.

Chikwere *abr ut* [chí-kwē-rē], (*var:* **Chikwelụ** [chí-kwē-lū]) God gave permission or allowed; God promised.

Chikwesịrị *ut* [chí-kwè-sì-rì], (*var:*
Chikwesịlị [chí-kwè-sì-lì])   God is
worthy. See this name in the Girls'
Names section.

Chima *abr* *ut* [chí-mā], (*var:*
Chukwuma(h) [chú-kwú-mā])   God
knows or God is all-knowing. God's
perfect knowledge of the universe as
well as the spirit world is central to Igbo
religious philosophy and worldview.
Each person's destiny is carefully hidden
away in the all-knowing mind of God
who directs the unfolding of this destiny
as He chooses. This belief in an all-
knowing God informed the practice of
swearing to an oath. Since He knows
whether one is telling the truth or not,
He was usually invoked in an oath as
means of settling a dispute, an
argument, or concluding a contract. The

gesture that signified someone was telling the truth was sticking out one's tongue, touching the tip of the tongue with the tip of the index finger of one's right hand, looking up to heaven as this index finger is pointed upward, signifying "I call heaven to witness that I'm telling the truth."

Chimaeze *ut* [chí-mā-é-zē], (*var*: **Chukwumaeze** [chú-kwú-mā-é-zē]) God fore-knows who will become a king.

Chimaobi *ut* [chí-mā-ó-bī] God knows the heart. The Igbo have a saying that goes the heart is like a bag, whose owner alone knows its content. This saying, of course, only applies to human beings, for God is omniscient and has a perfect knowledge of the human heart.

Chimereze *ut* [chí-mē-rē-é-zē]
Crowned by God.

Chimezie *sub ut* [chí-mē-zi-é], (*var*:
Mezie [mē-zi-é]) May God make
perfect.

Chinaecherem *ut* [chí-nā-é-chē-rém] God thinks about / for me. One
of the many Igbo names that
demonstrate reliance on God for
virtually all of life's existential
challenges, *Chinaecherem* celebrates
God as an incomparable, trustworthy
ally.

Chinaemerem *ut* [chí-nā-é-mē-rém],
(*var*: **Chinemerem**) [chí-né-mē-rém], God acts on my behalf. This is
another name that expresses reliance on
God.

Chinaenye *ut* [chí-nā-è-nyé], (*var*: **Chinenye** [chí-nē-nyé] or **Chukwunenye** [chú-kwú-nē-nyé]) God provides. The notion of God's provision for his creatures is strongly entrenched in Igbo philosophy. The Igbo gratefully recognize that everything they own comes from God as a special provision. As it was pointed out in the name *Chikwem*, this hard-held belief does not interfere with the Igbo work ethic and industry.

Chinaero *ut* [chí-nā-é-rō], (*var*: **Chinero** [chí-né-rō] or **Chinelo** [chí-né-lō]) God thinks about / for me. This name is a dialectic variant of *Chinaecherem* above.

Chinasa *ut* [chí-nā-á-sā] God answers (on my behalf). This deference to God as the spokesperson is typical of the Igbo who normally appeal to divine alliance and intervention, especially when faced with intractable existential threats or all-powerful adversaries. This name is a self-effacing response of parents who recognize their cause to be just and thus appeal to the all-knowing God to adjudicate on their behalf.

Chinatụ *ut* [chí-nā-á-tū] God decides (has the final verdict), God is the judge.

Chinaza *abr ut* [chí-nā-zá] God answers (prayers). This acknowledgement that God not only hears, but answers the prayers of those who believe in Him, is a direct expression of gratitude to God for His love and involvement in their lives. The parents whose daughter is named *Chinaza*, might have prayed specifically for a daughter, or generally for a child; or it could be they had prayed for deliverance from another existential situation in which God intervened.

Chinedu(m) *ut* [chí-nē-dú(m)] God is the (my) guide or leader. The journey through the rugged and dangerous terrains of life requires the leading of an all-knowing guide who is competent and strong enough to safely guide through this earthly journey.

Chinenye *abr ut* [chí-nē-nyé], (*var*: **Chukwunenye**) [chú-kwú- nē-nyé] God is the giver. This is a shortened form of *Chinenyendu,* God is the giver of life. Igbo religious philosophy is definite and unanimous in attributing life and human existence to God. Indeed, every Igbo acknowledges owing not only their life, but everything they possess to divine providence. *Chinenye* gives expression to this religious belief.

Chinkata *ut* [chi-n-kà-tà]   God is sovereign or God rules overall.

Chinọnso *ut* [chí-nō-n-só]   God is near. The belief in a personal God creates a sense of proximity, even intimacy between the Igbo and their God.

Chinọnye *sub ut* [chí-nō-nyé], (*var:* **Chukwunonye** [chú-kwú-nō-nyé] May God be (abide) with (me or us).

Chinụa *abr imp ut* [chí-nū-á] (*var:*
Chinụalụmọgụ [chí-nū-á-lúm-ò-gù] or
Chilụọrọmọgụ [chí-lū-ó-róm-ò-gù])
Let God fight for me or the battle is
God's.

Chinwe *abr ut* [chí-nwē] or [chí-nwè]
Belongs to God or is from God. Usually
the short form of longer names as in the
next six entries.

Chinweakụ *ut* [chí-nwē-à-kù]
Wealth belongs to (or comes from) God.

Chinweike *ut* [chí-nwē-í-ké] All
power belongs to God.

Chinweikpe *ut* [chí-nwé-í-kpé]
Judgment belongs to God.

Chinwendụ *ut* [chí-nwé-n-dʼū]   Life is from God or God is the source of life. See Chinenye above. *Chinwendụ* particularly expresses God's ownership of life, especially in the sense that this life is protectively hidden away in God. This name is therefore a declaration of the divine security enjoyed by the Igbo.

Chinweoke *ut* [chí-nwé-ò-kè]   The choice belongs to God.

Chinweụba [chí-nwē-ūbá]   Wealth belongs to God, meaning wealth comes from God.

Chinyere *abr* *ut* [chí-nyè-rè] Endowed by God.

Chinyereze *ut* [chí-nyè-rè-é-zē] Kingship or royalty is bestowed by God.

Chioma *nom phr* [chí-ó-má] Good God, good fortune or good providence. *Chioma* is a celebration of God's goodness toward His creation.

Chisom *ut* [chí-só-m] God is with me, or God is on my side. No adversary can be so formidable as to withstand God. So when Igbo parents declare that God is on their side, the implication is that they are invincible. By giving their son this name, the parents are boasting of the unfailing quality of divine protection.

Chizara(m) *ut* [chí-zā-rā-(m) God answered (my prayer), (me).

Chizuru(m) *ut* [chí-zū-rū-(m)], (*var*: **Chukwuzuru(m)** [chú-kwú-zū-rū-(m)] God is my all and all in all. Literally, God is all I need or God is sufficient. See *Onyenachi*.

Chuka *abr* *ut* [chú-kā], (*var*: **Chukwuka** [chú-kwú-kā]) See *Chika* above.

Chukwu *n* [chú-kwú] God. Literally great God, *Chi ukwu* as opposed to mini-gods and deities.

Chukwudị *ut* [chú-kwú-dī], (*var*: **Chidị** [chí-dī] God is or there is God.

Chukwuemeka *ut* [chú-kwú-ē-mé-ká], (*var*: **Emeka** [è-mé-ká]) Thanks be to God. Literally: God has done marvelously well.

Chukwuezi *nom ut* [chú-kwú-ē-zī]
The God of the family.

Chukwukere *ut* [chú-kwú-kè-rè]
Created by God.

Chukwuma(h) *ut* [chú-kwú-mā],
(*var*: **Chima** [chí-mā] God is all-knowing.

Chukwunọnye *sub ut* [chú-kwú-nō-nyé] May God be (abide) with (me / us). Same name as *Chinọnye*.

D

Dibịa *n* [dí-bī-ā] Doctor (*trad. med.*), also chief priest of an oracle or diviner.

Dike *n* [dī-ké] A powerful man; a great man or a man of great authority. A warrior or hero.

Dimgba *n* [dí-m-gbá] Master wrestler.

Dimkpa *n* [dí-m-kpā] A man of great strength, courage and ability.

Diọka *n* [dí-ò-kà] Master specialist in a particular trade.

E

Ebekunwanne *abr ut* [è-bé-kū-nwá-n-nē]   One cries out only to one's kinsfolk. A proud and secretive people, the Igbo nonetheless confide in one another. The social philosophy of communal affinity makes individual struggle and tribulation a family or even clan affair. As the Igbo proverb goes, *"Imi n'anya bụ nwanne; anya bewa akwa, imi esoro ya bewa"* (the eye and the nose are siblings; when one hurts, the other cries in sympathy). Any struggle one cannot shoulder alone is usually brought to the attention of one's kith and kin, whose responsibility it is to put their heads together and find a solution to the problem.

Ebekuo *abr ut* [é-bé-kū-ó] When one cries out (a ready and attentive ear comes to an aid.)

Ebere *n* [è-bé-rē] Mercy.

Eberechi *nom phr* [è-bé-rē-chī], (*var*: **Eberechukwu**) [è-bé-rē-chú-kwú] God's mercy, kindness and com-passion.

Ebochi *abr ut* [é-bō-ò-chí], (*var*: **Egbochi**) [é-bō-ò-chí] danger is averted when the gods are appeased.

Ebọgụ *abr ut* [é-bō-ó-ò-gù], (*var*: **Egbọgụ**) [é-gbō-ó-ò-gù] When peace is made between warring parties, enmity and animosity cease.

Ebube *n* [è-bù-bè]   Glory.

Ebubechi *nom phr* [è-bù-bé-chī], (*var*: **Ebubechukwu**) [è-bù-bé-chú-kwú]   God's glory.

Echefula *imp ut* [é-chē-fū-lā]   Do not forget (*var*: **Echefulachi**) [é-chē-fū-lā-chí]   Do not forget God.

Echewaọzọ or **Echewaozor** *abr ut* [é-chē-wá-ō-zō], (*var*: **Echewaọdọ** or **Echewaodor** [é-chē-wá-ō-dō])   When you prepare to face one thing, something else crops up.

Egbuchulam *abr ut* [é-gbū-chū-lām], (*var*: **Onwụegbuchulam** [ó-nwú- é-gbū-chū-lām])   May I not die an untimely death.

93

Egbulefu *abr ut* [è-gbú-lé-fū] Persecuted unjustly. The meaning of this name is self-explanatory. The parents who give this name to their son see themselves as victims of unjust mistreatment and oppression from their adversaries. The implication of this name is that the victims will be vindicated by their innocence, as divine justice will protect the innocent from persecutors.

Egedeụzụ *nom phr* [è-gè-dé-ù-zù] Warrior. An overly aggressive and ruth-lessly competitive person.

Egeọnụ *abr ut* [é-gē-é-ó-nū] Giving in to public opinion could undermine you indecisive, meaning that taking advice from any Dick, Tom and Harry could sabotage / jeopardize the success of an operation.

Egwuatụ *nom phr* [é-gwū-á-tū] Fearless, intrepid or invincible.

Ehiemere *abr ut* [è-hì-é-mè-rè]   The day of accomplishment or resolution, a historic day.

Ehilegbu *abr ut* [è-hì-lé-gbū]   The day an innocent person is killed or persecuted, may I not be around, meaning God forbid that I take part in killing (persecuting) an innocent person.

Ejiakonye *inter ut* [è-jì-á-ká-ō-nyē] Whose hands are being held back? In other words: 'am I standing in anyone's way?'

Ejidike *abr ut* [é-jī-dí-kē]   You boast when you have a great man.

Ejiekpe *abr ut* [è-jì-è-kpé]   A child whose birth serves as peace treaty. As stated in the entry for Ekwubiri, childlessness breeds intolerable angst among members of a family. This situation sometimes devolves into a feud and cold war with the parties involved feeling desolate that the family line has reached a dead end. A child born into this situation could be named Ejiekpe, as all parties to the feud normally join together in celebration of the new birth.

Ejike *abr ut* [é-jī-í-ké]   Brute force or show of strength is not a panacea for the ills of the world.

Ejiribe *abr ut* [é-jī-rí-bʲè]   If all of one's hope is placed on folks, then disappointment is near.

Ejitụ *abr ut* [é-jī-tú]   To be held in trust temporarily. Such was the high infant mortality rate in those days that babies were not expected to survive onto their first birthday. Hence the name *Ejitụ*, which literally means: let's hold him or her in our hands for a while. Parents who have repeatedly had this experience were more likely to give this name to their newborn, which smacks of resignation to fate. Male children from such families were not circumcised in infancy and every effort was made not to expose them to any dangers or health hazards. Some of those parents would not even as much as allow their children to play with their peers for fear of accidental death.

Eke *n* i. [è-ké]   *Eke* market day. This name is given to achild born on the *Eke* market day.

ii. [é-kè]   When pronounced this way, *Eke* means fate, fortune or destiny. Echeruo calls *Eke* "the deity that allots fate" (45).

Ekechi *nom phr* [é-kē-é-chī]   Fate, fortune or destiny allotted by God.

Ekejiụba *ut* [é-kè-jì-ù-bá]   Wealth is determined or allotted by fate or destiny.

Ekele *n* [è-kè-lé], (also **Ekene** [è-kè-né])   Greeting(s) or thanks.

Ekelediṛichukwu *ut* [è-kè-lé-dì-rí-chú-kwú], (*var*: **Ekenediḷichukwu** [è-kè-né-dì-rí-chú-kwú]   Thanks be to God.

Ekeleme *abr ut*   [é-kē-é-lē-mè] Death overthrows human plans and efforts. Meaning that after you have planned out all the course of an action, then suddenly it is upended by death.

Ekeọma *nom phr*   i.   [è-ké-ó-má] Good *Eke* market day.

    ii. [è-kè-ó-má]   Good or favourable fate or destiny.

Ekwubiri *imp ut* [é-kwú-bī-rí]   Let all mouths be stopped. It is generally expected that after one year of marriage, a couple should be blessed with a child. If this time lapses without any sign of pregnancy, tongues normally start to wag. When this couple eventually have a child, and a male child at that, they may choose to sue for all the gossip to stop by naming their son *Ekwubiri*, meaning: 'Enough of all that talk!'

Ekwueme   *nom phr* [è-kwú-ē-mé] A man of his words.

Elendụ *abr ut* [è-lè-n-ɗù] We accept whatever lot life has allotted to us.

Elenwoke *abr ut* [è-lè-nwó-kē]   A man as he is supposed to be.

Elewachi *imp ut* [é-lé-wá-chī]   Let's wait and see what God will do.

Eluwa(h) *n* [é-lú-ū-wā]   The world, the earth or the universe; also used metonymically to refer to life on earth.

Emedo(h) *abr ut* [é-mé-d̀ó-ó]
After reconciliation faces light up.

Emeka *abr ut*   [è-mé-ká], (also: **Chukwuemeka**   [chú-kwú-ē-mé-ká]) Thanks be to God.

Emelogu *abr ut*   [è-mé-ló-gū] Uprightness being my watch word, I will always be vindicated. The common saying, '***Ejikwa m ogu***' (I will be vindicated) is used by the Igbo to assert their guiltlessness during the adjudication of cases in which they are sure of being vindicated.

Emenike *abr ut* [é-mē-nī-kē] Good leadership is not by brute force and demonstration of power. A leader does not force himself on his followers.

Emezuo *abr ut* [é-mé-zū-ó], (*var:* **Emezue** [é-mé- ū-zé]) When a promise is fulfilled, there is a sense of accomplishment. Promise-keeping is of paramount importance in Igbo interpersonal dynamics. This ideal is so prized that beloved civic leaders are sometimes fondly called '*Ọ kaa, O mee*': a man of his words. **Emezuo** is also a short form of *Chiemezuo*.

Eṅeogwe *abr ut* [è-nó-gwē], (*var:* **Eṅogwe** [è-nó-gwē] A log or fallen tree is generally crossed at its lowest point.

Enyereibe *abr ut* [è-nyè-rè-í-bʲē]   If I relied on folks to deliver my portion, I would be without any.

Enyi *n*   i. [é-nyī]   Friend.
     ii. [é-nyí]   Elephant.

Enyinna *nom phr* [é-nyī-n-nā], (*var* **Enyinnaya**) [é-nyī-n-nā-yá] Father's friend.

Enyioma(h) *nom phr*   [é-nyī-ómá] Good friend.

Erondụ *abr ut* [è-rò-n-dù]   A thought or reflection on life.

Eze(h) *n* [é-zē]   A king. As in the name *Adaeze* in the Girls' Names section, kingship among the Igbo is not hereditary. As a result the name *Eze* doesn't confer royalty on the child, but only expresses his parents' aspiration.

Ezeala *nom phr* [é-zē-à-là]   King of the domain. Literally, king of the land. The dream of parents is for their children to rise to a position of prominence, to grow up to be a ruler.

Ezeamaka *ut* [é-zē-à-má-ká]   The king is of an unparalleled beauty.

Ezebuoke *ut* [é-zē-bú-ò-kè] Destined to be a king; or kingship or royalty is my lot or portion.

Ezechukwu *nom phr* [é-zē-chú-kwú] A God-ordained king.

Ezeji *nom phr* [é-zē-jí]   A man wealthy in yams, the chief cash crop of traditional Igbo society. The quantity of yams a man had used to be a measure of his riches. After harvest, yams were stored in barns until the next planting season. Any man who had ten or more barns full of yams was inducted into the **Ezeji** society, comprising as the name suggests, men who have distinguished themselves through the abundance of yams they have produced for society. *Ezeji* as a name is therefore an aspiration on the part of parents that their son will become a member of this exclusive group of title-holders.

Ezekwesiri *nom phr* [é-zē-kwè-sì-rì], (*var*: **Ezekwesili** [é-zē-kwè-sì-rì]) Worthy to be a king.

Ezenwa(h) *nom phr* [é-zē-nwá] Kingly child.

Ezeọha *nom phr* [é-zē-ò-hà] The people's king.

Ezeudo *nom phr* [é-zē-ū-dò̄] King of peace.

Ezeugo *nom phr* [é-zē-ù-gò] Distinguished king; also a title of nobility.

Ezidionye *nom phr* [é-zí-dí-ō-nyē] Good husband.

Ezinwanne *nom phr* [é-zí-nwā-n-nē] Beloved brother.

Ezinwoke *nom phr* [é-zí-nwó-kē] Good man child.

Eziọma *nom phr* [è-zí-ó-má] Good family, household or clan.

Eziuche *nom phr* [é-zí-ú-chē] Good thought or wise counsel.

Eziugwu *n* i. [é-zí-ú-gwū] Good hill.
                 ii. [é-zí-ū-gwū] Good respect.

Ezuruike *imp ut* [é-zū-rú-í-kē], (*var*: **Ezulike** [é-zū-lú-í-kē]) Let me / us enjoy some rest.

G / I / J

Gịnịgaeme [gí-nī-gà-è-mé] Literally: 'what will happen?' This is the self-confident rhetorical question: 'who has the audacity to raise an eyebrow?'

Ibe(h) *n* [í-bʰē] Folk, companion, mate.

Ibeabụghịchi *ut* [í-bʰē-á-bū-ghī-chī], (*var*: **Ibeabụchi** [í-bʰē-á-bū-chī] or **Ibeawụchi** [í-bʰē-á-wū-chī]) Folks are not God; meaning: 'My destiny is not in the hands of fellow human beings, but in God's hands.'

Ibegbula(m) *ut* [í-bʰē-é-gbū-lá(m)], (*var*: **Ibegbuna(m)** [í-bʰē-é-gbū-ná(m)] May my folks not kill me.

Ibekwe(m) *abr ut* [í-bʰē-kwé-m] If folks let me alone.

Ibenegbu *ut* [í-bʰē-nē-gbú] Your folks are the very ones who actions kill or betray you.

Ibezim *abr ut* [í-bʰè-zí-m], (*var:*
Ibezimakọ [í-bʰè-zí-mā-kō], or
Zimakọ [zí-mā-kō]) As folks teach
me some clever life lessons I am made
all the wiser. This name underlines the
importance of customary education in a
society where instruction took place
informally in the course of interpersonal
exchanges and not in schools which
were inexistent in pre-literate Igbo
society.

Idika *n* [ì-dì-ká] A very strong
person. This name also means patience
is of utmost importance.

Ifeanachọ *nom phr* [í-fé-á-nā-chó] or
Ifanachọ [í-fá-nā-chó]; (*var:*
Iheanachọ [í-hé-á-nā-chó] or
Ihanachọ [í-há-nā-chó]) Our
ambition or the object of our pursuit.

Ifeanyị *ut* [í-fé-á-nyī], (*var*: **Iheanyị** [í-hé-á-nyī], **Iheanyịchi** [í-hé-á-nyī-chí], **Iheanyịchukwu**, [í-hé-á-nyī-chú-kwú] or **Ifeanyịchukwu** [í-fé-á-nyī-chú-kwú]   Literally: nothing is too difficult for God. God's omnipotence and omniscience are central to Igbo religious philosophy. Because God's power and knowledge are infinite, He is able to govern our complex universe and the unfolding of each life on earth. *Ifeanyị* is a celebration of this divine attribute.

Igbomalụ *imp ut*   [ì-gbò-mà-lú] Let it be clear to all. Let the whole world know. The completing part of this name (i.e. what should be clear to all or what everybody should know) depends on the particular circumstance of the family that give this name to their son.

110

Igbokwe *abr ut* [ì-gbò-kwé]   If my people (folks) would permit me.

Igwe *n*   [í-gwē]   Title of nobility. Chief.

Igwedinma *nom phr*   [í-gwé-dī-n-mā]   Heaven is a good abode.

Iheanetu *nom phr*   [í-hé-á-nē-tú] Our ambition or the object of our pursuit. This name means the same thing as *Ifeanacho* or *Iheanacho*.

Ihechi *nom phr*   [ì-hé-chī], (*var*: **Ihechukwu**) [ì-hè-chú-kwú]   Divine light.

Ihechimere *nom phr* [í-hé-chí-mē-rē] A task performed by God or an act of God.

Ihejiato̟(r) *nom phr* [í-hé-é-jī-à-tó] Source of shared joy.

Ihejio̟nu̟eme *nom phr* [í-hé-é-jī-ó-nú-ē-mé] Literally: "what the mouth is, or words are, capable of doing," meaning the power of the mouth or words.

Ihejirika *nom phr* [í-hé-é-jī-rī-ká] Supremacy or excellency.

Ihekwoaba *nom phr* [í-hé-é-kwō-à-bʰá] Something to brag about or reason to boast.

Iheme *abr ut* [í-hé-é-mē]   Everything happens for a reason or no occurrence is fortuitous.

Iheọma(mere) *ut* [í-hé-ó-má-(mē-rē)] Something good happened.

Iheọnụnekwu *nom phr* [í-hé-ó-nú-nē-kwú]   The things people say.

Ihesiaba *abr ut*   [í-hé-é-sī-à-bʰ á] Something to brag about or reason to boast. This name is a dialectal variant of *Ihekwoaba*.

Ihesiụlọ *abr ut* [í-hé-sī-ú-lò]   What we are dealing with originates from home (household) or the family.

Iheukwu *abr ut*   [í-hé-ú-kwú], (*var:* **Iheukwumere**)   [í-hé-ú-kwú-mē-rē]

Something great happened. This name heralds the new-born's auspicious entry into the world as well as prophesying his greatness.

Ịhụnanya *n* [í-hū-nà-á-nyá]   Love.

Ịhụnanyachi *nom phr* [í-hū-nà-á-nyá-chí] (*var*: Ịhụnanyachukwu [í-hū-nà-á-nyá-chú-kwú])   God's love.

Ijendụ *nom phr* [í-jē-n-dụ̀ ū]   Life's journey.

Ijeoma *nom phr* [í-jē-ó-má]   Good journey. The journey referred to here is generally that of marriage. The couple each took a journey, literally, toward each other: the man to his bride's hometown, and the bride to her groom's home. When the marriage is blessed with a child, the couple has the opportunity to declare their journey a blessing and a success, *Ijeoma*. This name is also given to a child born when his mother or parents were on their way to somewhere.

Ike *n* [í-ké] Strength or power.

Ikebuaku *ut* [í-ké-bū-à-kù] Strength or power is wealth. Also health is wealth.

Ikechi *nom phr* [í-ké-chī], (*var*: **Ikechukwu** [í-ké-chú-kwú]) God's Power.

Ikedinachi *ut* [í-ké-dī-nā-chí] There is power in God's Name (God is a repository of power)

Ikpeazụ *nom* *phr* [í-kpé-à-zù] Judgement or trial in absentia; secret trial or verdict.

Ikpechi *nom phr* [í-kpé-chī], (*var:* **Ikpechukwu** [í-kpé-chū-kwū]) God's verdict or judgement.

Ikonne *nom* *phr* [í-kó-n-nē] Mother's boyfriend or concubine.

Ikwu *n* [í-kwú] Kindred or kinsfolk.

Ikwuakọ *abr* *ut* [í-kwú-á-kō], (*var:* **Ikwuakọlam** [í-kwú-á-kō-lām]) May I never lack kinsfolk.

Imo(h) *n* [í-mō] River.

Iro(h) *n* [í-ró] Enmity, hatred.

Iroegbu(lam) *sub ut* [í-ró-é-gbū(lám)], (*var*: **Iroegbu(nam)** [í-ró-é-gbū(nám)] May I not die in the hands of my enemy.

Irọha *nom phr* [í-ró-ò-hà] Community-wide hatred or enmity.

Irondi *abr ut* [í-ró-n-dì]   There is hatred or enmity even at home.

Iwejụọ *abr ut* [í-wé-jú-ó]   May all the anger now subside or dissipate. In other words: it is time to bury the hatchet; the warring factions should forgive and forget.

Iwu *n* [ì-wú]   Law, edict, decree or rules. Why would a couple give this name to their child? Laws in Igboland are sacrosanct and non-negotiable. Although they were not written, they keep the society in check and intact and are at the heart of the very definition of social cohesion and judicial sanctions called **omenala** or **omenani** (culture).

Iwuagwụ *nom phr* [ì-wú-á-gwū] The laws or rules of a deity.

Iwuala *nom phr* [ì-wú-à-là] The laws, edicts or decrees of the land, *legem terrae*. Also, by extension, the laws, edicts or decrees of **Ala** the earth goddess.

Iwuchukwu *nom phr* [ì-wú-chú-kwú] God's law(s), edict or decree.

Iwumụọ *nom phr* [ì-wú-mú-ō] The laws, edicts or decrees of the spirit world, deity or ancestors.

Iwundu *nom phr* [ì-wú-n-dʰù] The laws of life.

Iwuọha *nom phr* [ì-wú-ō-hā] The laws of the community.

Izu *n* [ì-zù] Wisdom.

Izuchi *nom phr* [ì-zú-chī], *(var: Izuchukwu)* [ì-zù-chú-kwú] God's wisdom.

Izundu *nom phr* [ì-zù-n-dʰū] Wisdom for living.

Izuọgụ [ì-zú-ò-gʰù] War plan, or strategy.

Jaachike *imp ut* [já-á-chī-ī-kē] Praise God for His power.

Jideaka *imp ut* [jì-dé-á-kā]   Hold on or hang on.

K / M

Kalụ *n* [ká-á-lū] or **Kamalụ** [ká-má-lū], (*var*: **Kanụ** [ká-á-nū])   A child dedicated to the god of thunder.

Kanayọ *abr imp ut* [kà-á-ná-ā-yó] Let's keep praying or beseeching. This name could be given to a child whose parents have experienced the death of an infant child or more, and are praying that their son will live and not die; it could also be that the mother experienced some difficulty during pregnancy or at the birth of her child and the prayer is for the mother's survival. The name could also be given to a baby boy or girl whose grandparents – paternal or maternal – have been experiencing some life's challenges.

Kelechi *imp ut* [kè-lé-é-chī], (*var:* **Kelechukwu** [kè-lé-é-chú-kwú]) Give thanks to God or thanks be to God.

Madụ *n* [má-ɗù] Human person(s).

Madụabụchi *ut* [má-ɗù-á-bū-chī] (*var:* **Madụabụghịchi**) [má-ɗù-á-bū-ghī-chī] People or human beings are not God. Meaning that people can do, say or think whatever they would, what is important is God's perspective.

Madụbuike *ut* [má-ɗù-bú-í-ké]
People are a source of strength.

Madụbuiṅe *ut* [má-ɗù-bú-í-ṅē]
People are a source of pride.

Madụfọrọ *ut* [má-ɗù-fó-ró]   There
is someone or there are people left.

Madụkakụ *abr ut* [má-ɗù-ká-à-kù],
(*var*: **Madụka** [má-ɗù-ká] A person
is worth more than wealth.

Matachi *imp ut* [mà-tá-chī], (*var*:
Marachi [mà-rá-chī])   Acknowledge
or recognize God.

Mba(h) *n* [m-bʲá]   Rebuke,
admonition; boasting or threat.

Mbakọgu *ut* [m-bʲ á-á-kā-ò-gù], (*var*: Mbakaghịọgu [m-bá-á-kā-ghí-ò-gù] A rebuke is less dangerous than a battle or war.

Mbamalụ *ut* [m-bà-mà-lú] A society has faith in its own ethos, ideals and values.

Mbaọma *nom phr* [m-bà-ó-má], (*var*: Mbọma [m-bó-má]) (A) good race, people or country.

Mbaọnụ *nom phr* [m-bʲá-ó-nū], (*var*: Mbọnụ) [m-bʲó-nū] Unfounded boasting. Also, empty threat.

Metụ (*var*: Metuh) *abr imp ut* [mè-tú] Uncommon situations reveal people's true colour. In other words, you can only learn people's true character by interacting with them in their unguarded moments.

N

Nchekwube *n* [n-chē-kwú-bú]   Great expectation, hope or trust. It is evident that the parents who give this name to their child are, through it, praying for and prophesying a great future for him or her.

Ndidi *n*   [n-dì-dì]   Patience or endurance. The Igbo believe this virtue conquers all things and are quick to urge and prescribe patience to anyone who is facing a trying situation.

Ndubuaku *ut* [n-ɗū-bú-à-kù] Life is wealth.

Ndubueze *ut* [n-ɗū-bú-é-zē] Life is supreme. Literally: life is king, this name also means that you have to be alive to be king.

Ndubuisi *ut* [n-ɗū-bú-í-sí] Life is paramount, meaning: life is the principal thing.

Ndubuka *ut* [n-ɗū-bú-ú-kā] Life has its inherent issues and problems.

Ndubuoke *ut* [n-ɗū-bú-ò-kè] Life is a gift. This name literally means that life has been allotted to each person as their own share of divine generosity.

Ndụka *abr ut* [n-ɗū-ká]   Life is paramount or life is the most important thing.

Ndụkakụ *ut* [n-ɗū-ká-à-kù]   Life is worth more than riches.

Ndụkanma *ut* [n-ɗū-ká-n-má]   Life is priceless or invaluable.

Ndụkaụba *ut* [n-ɗū-ká-ú-bá]   Life is worth more than wealth.

Ndụkwe *abr ut* [n-ɗū-kwé]   If life permits.

Ngọzi *n* [n-gó-zí]   Blessing.

Ngọzichi *nom phr* [n-gó-zí-chí], (*var*: **Ngọzichukwu** [n-gó-zí-chū-kwū])   God's blessing.

Ngozika *abr ut* [n-gó-zí-kā]   Blessing is of paramount importance.

Ngwaba *abr ut* [n-gwà-á-bā] No one in society gets rich through slothfulness or by idling away their time.

Ngwaekwe *abr ut*   [n-gwà-é-kwē] Folks do not let or permit (a certain thing from happening), or folks forbid.

Ngwakwe *abr ut* [n-gwà-kwé]   If folks or society let or permit me.

Ngwaziem *abr ut* [n-gwà-zí-ém] Folks or society are my school of life's experiences.

Njideaka *nom phr* [n-jì-ɗé-á-kā] Assurance and confidence. *Njideaka* literally refers to 'having a firm grip on something'.

Njideka *ut* [n-jì-d́é-kā]   There is a more abiding assurance in ownership than in pursuit. This name roughly translates the axiomatic expression 'a bird in hand is worth two in the bush' and is analogous to *Nkemjika* below.

Njọkụ *n* [n-jó-kū]   Dedicated to the yam god. This is one of Igbo names that indicate devotion to a deity.

Nkem *pos pron* [n-kè-m]   Mine or my own. Often the shortened form of the next three names of which it is the prefix.

Nkemakọlam *sub ut* [n-kè-m-á-kō-lām]) May my share always belong to me.

Nkemdịrịm *sub ut* [n-kè-m-dì-rí-m], (*var*: **Nkemdịlịm** [n-kè-m-dì-lí-m] May what is mine always be mine.

Nkemka *abr ut* [n-kè-m-kā], (*var*: **Nkemjika** [n-kè-m-jī-ká]) I have the best part or share.

Nkeonyere *abr ut* [n-kè-ó-nyè-rè] Whatever gift He (God) gives is perfect.

Nkume or **Nkumeh** *n* [n-kú-mē] Stone or rock. Fortitude and courage, resilience and valour: these are very highly prized attributes of the typical Igbo male which are encapsulated in the name *Nkume*.

Nkwachi(kwere) *nom phr* [n-kwà-chí-(kwè-rè)]   God's promise. Literally: promise made by God.

Nkwọcha *nom phr* [n-kwó-chá] Light-skinned son (male child) born on an *Nkwọ* market day.

Nmezi *n* [n-mé-zí]   Doing what is right and proper, or doing the right thing.

Nnabụike *ut* [n-nā-bú-í-ké]   Father is the source of courage.

Nnabụiṅe *ut* [n-nā-bú-í-ṅè]   Father is the source of pride.

Nnadozie *sub ut* [n-nà-dò-zi-e]   May father organize and preserve.

Nnaemeka *ut* [n-nà-é-mé-ká]   All thanks to Father or Father has done exceedingly well.

Nnamdị *ut*   [n-nàm-dī], (*var:* **Nnadị** [n-nà-dì])   My father lives on. *Nna m dị ndụ* is the full name and literally means '*my father is alive,*' clearly showing that this name could be a direct reference to the reincarnation of the father.

Nnamụrụ *nom phr*   [n-nà-mù-rù] Begotten of his father in other words, his father's son.

Nnanna *n* [n-nà-n-nà]   Grandfather. This name is given to a boy who is believed to be the reincarnation of his grandfather. See *Nnenne* in the Girls'

Names section for feminine equivalent of this name for girls.

Nnọchiri *abr int ut* [n-nò-chì-rì]   Am I standing in anybody's way? Understand: am I blocking or impeding anyone's progress?

Nnọdịm *abr imp ut*   [n-nò-dí-m] Let me alone or allow me to be myself.

Nnụfọrọole *abr int ut* [n-nù-fò-rò-ò-lé], (*var*: **Nnụfọrole** [n-nù-fò-rò-lé]) What did I not hear? Meaning: I had an earful. See *Anụbiri* above.

Nọnyerem *imp ut* [nò-nyé-ré-m] Abide, stand with me or support me.

Nwaba *n* [nwá-ā-bā]   A free-born Aba native.

Nwachukwu *nom phr* [nwá-chú-kwú]
Child of deity, meaning dedicated to a
deity.

Nwadigo *ut* [nwá-ā-dī-gō]   I / We
now have a child.

Nwadike *nom phr* [nwá-dí-kē]   Son
of a great man or son of a warrior.

Nwadịnma *nom phr* [nwá-dī-n-mà]
A goodly child.

Nwadire *nom phr* [nwá-dī-ì-rè]   A
smart, resourceful child.

Nwaeke *nom phr* i. [nwá-ē-kē], (*var*
Nweke [nwá-ē-kē])   A child born on
the *Eke* market day.

ii. [nwá-é-kè] A child of destiny or fate.

Nwaeze *nom phr* [nwá-é-zē], (*var*: **Nweze** [nwé-zē] A prince.

Nwafọ (*var*: **Nwafor**) *nom phr* [nwá-à-fò] A child born on the *Afọ* market day.

Nwagbara *nom phr* [nwá-á-gbā-rā] A child dedicated to a deity.

Nwagụ *nom phr* [nwá-á-gū] A tiger cub.

Nwaigwe *nom phr* [nwá-í-gwē], (*var*: **Nwigwe** [nwí-gwē] or **Wigwe** [wí-gwē]) A heavenly child. Also: a child dedicated to the Sky god.

Nwaiwu *nom phr* [nwá-ī-wū]   A child who upholds law and order.

Nwakanma *ut* [nwá-kā-n-má]   A child is priceless. This name also means: I would rather have a child, or a child is of the greatest value.

Nwakọlam *sub ut* [nwá-kō-lám] May I never go childless.

Nwakọrọ *ut* [nwá-kō-rō]   Children are scarce, or children are unique.

Nwala *nom phr* [nwá-à-là], (*var*: **Wala** [wá-à-là] or **Nwanị** [nwá-à-nì])   A free-born son; a child dedicated to *Ala* or *Anị* the Earth goddess.

Nwamaka *ut* [nwá-ā-mā-kā]   A child who is the epitome of beauty. See this name in the Girls' Names section.

Nwamkpa *nom phr* [nwá-m-kpà] The child who fills a great need; also: an answer to prayer.

Nwanganga *nom phr* [nwá-n-gà-n-gà]   A child who is the source of pride.

Nwankwọ *nom phr* [nwá-n-kwó]   A child born on an *Nkwọ* market day.

Nwanna *nom phr* [nwá-n-nā] Kinsman.

Nwaọba *nom phr* [nwá-ó-bʰā]   A hatchling (baby crocodile); also child of the stream (Echeruo, 132).

Nwaọbasị *nom phr* [nwá-ò-bà-sì]   A child dedicated to *Ọbasị*, the supreme god.

Nwaọbịa *nom phr* [nwá-ó-bʰī-à]   A guest child. This name is not, as some may think, a term of alienation. It speaks to the notion of the spirit-child, *ogbanje*, who chooses a cyclical reincarnation. A male child suspected of being an *ogbanje* could be named *Nwaọbịa* as a term of endearment intended to persuade him to break the cycle of reincarnation and stay with the family.

Nwaobilọ or Nwaobilor *nom phr* [nwá-ó-bī-ló]), (also: often shortened to Obilọ [ó-bī-ló], Obialọ (Obialor) [ó-bī-ā-ló] or Obiayọ [ó-bī-ā-yó]) Child of comfort or consolation.

Nwaobodo *nom phr* [nwá-ò-bò-dò], (*var*: **Nwobodo** [nwá-ò-bò-dò]) A free-born son or native son; an identical name to the first meaning of *Nwala* or *Nwanị* above. However, while *Nwala* or *Nwanị* may be dedicated to the Earth goddess, this is not the case with *Nwaobodo*.

Nwaogu *nom phr* [nwá-ó-gū], (*var*: **Nwogu** [nwó-gū] or **Wogu** [wó-gū]) A child who is the embodiment of uprightness, integrity or probity. See *Ogu* below.

Nwaọgụ *nom phr* [nwá-ò-gù], (*var*: **Nwọgụ** [nwò-gù] or **Wọgụ** [wò-gù]) Born in the middle of a war. War here should be understood both in the literal and figurative senses of the word, especially in the latter as this name could give an insight into the interpersonal dynamics of family relations.

Nwaogwugwu *nom phr* [nwá-ò-gwù-gwù], (*var*: **Nwogwugwu** [nwó-gwù-gwù] A child dedicated to *Ogwugwu*, the fertility goddess (Echeruo, 123).

Nwaojii *nom phr* [nwá-ó-jí-ī] Black child.

Nwaokike *nom phr* [nwá-ò-kì-kè] A child who is the embodiment of a creative genius.

Nwaokocha *nom phr* [nwá-ó-kō-ó-chá], (*var*: **Nwokocha** [nwó-kō-ó-chá] or **Okocha** [ò-kó-chá]) Light-skinned son (male child).

Nwaokojii *nom phr* [nwá-ó-kō-ō-jíī], (*var*: **Nwokeojii** [nwó-kē-ō-jíī] or **Nwokojii** [nwó-kō-ō-jíī] Black son (male child).

Nwaokoukwu *nom phr* [nwá-ó-kō-ū-kwū] A big male child. The adjective *big* could refer to both size and worth.

Nwaosu *nom phr* [nwá-ō-sū], (*var*: **Nwosu** [nwó-sū]) A child dedicated to the service of the **osu** deity; also a descendant of the **osu** caste.

Nwaulo [nwá-ú-lò], (*var*: **Nwulo** [nwú-lò] or **Nw(a)ulo(r)**) Home boy. Also refers to a male child whose birth took place at home.

Nweke *nom phr* i. [nwē-ké], (*var*: **Nwaeke** [nwá-ē-ké]) A child born on the **Eke** market day.

ii. [nwá-é-kè] When pronounced this way, *Nwaeke* means child of fate, fortune or destiny. See the name *Eke*.

Nworie *nom phr* [nwó-rī-ē], (*var*: **Nwaorie** [nwá-ó-rī-ē]) A child born on the *Orie* market day.

Nwauke *nom phr* [nwá-ù-kè] A child of destiny.

Nze *n* [n-zè] A chief or nobleman. Also a traditional title of nobility. Given to a child at birth, this name, just like *Eze*, only expresses the parents' aspiration and doesn't confer any nobility on its bearer.

Nzeakọ *abr imp ut* [n-zè-á-kō], (*var*: Nzeakọlam [n-zè-á-kō-lām] May I never lack an *Nze* or a noblemen.

Nzube *n* [n-zù-bé] Intention, counsel, judgement or will.

Nzubechi *nom phr* [n-zù-bé-chī], (Nzubechukwu [n-zù-bé-chú-kwú]) God's intention, judgement or will.

O / Ọ

Ọbaji *nom phr* [ó-bʲá-jī] A barn of yams. See the name *Ezeji* in this present section for the economic significance of yams in traditional Igbo society.

Ọbasị *n* [ò-bà-sì]   God. This is one of the names of Igbo deity.

Obenwa *nom phr*   [ó-bé-nwā], (*var*: Oberenwa   [ó-bé-ré-nwā])   Little child.

Obi *n* i. [ò-bí] Household. Also royal title (*Ọnịcha*), but just like *Eze* and *Nze*, doesn't confer royalty on the child.

  ii. [ó-bī]   Heart; disposition or temperament.

Obiakọ or Obiakor *abr imp ut* [ò-bí-á-kō], (*var*: Obiakọlam   [ò-bí-á-kō-lām] or Obiakọnam   [ò-bí-á-kō-nām]) May I never lack a household or family.

Obialọ or Obialor [ó-bī-à-ló], (*var*: Obiayo [ó-bī-à-yó]) I/We have now been comforted or "what a relief!"

referring to the consolation and relief the birth of a son brings.

Obidike *nom phr* i. [ó-bī-dí-kē] The heart of a powerful man, a great man or a warrior.

ii. [ò-bí-dí-kē] The household of a powerful man, a great man or a warrior.

Obidinma *nom phr* i. [ó-bī-dí-n-mā] A good heart.

ii. [ò-bí-dí-n-mā] A good household or lineage.

Obiechina *imp ut* [ò-bí-é-chī-ná], (*var*: **Obiechila** [ò-bí-é-chī-lá]) May the family name, lineage or clan never come to an end. *Obiechina* is analogous to *Amaefula*.

Obiefuna *imp ut*   i.   [ò-bí-é-fū-nā],
(*var*: **Obiefula** [ò-bí-é-fū-lā]) May the
family name, lineage or clan never come
to an end, as in *Obiechina* above.

   ii. [ó-bì-é-fū-nā] or [ó-bì-é-fū-lā]
Be courageous or do not lose hope.

Obieze *nom phr*   i.   [ó-bí-é-zè]   The
king's palace.

   ii. [ó-bì-é-zè] A noble heart like
that of a king.

Obigwe *nom phr*   i.   [ó-bī-í-gwē]   A
heart disposed toward heaven.

   ii. [ó-bī-í-gwè] A heart of steel.

Obinna *nom phr* i. [ó-bì-n-nà]   The
object of his father's love or affection
(heart). Literally, father's heart.

   ii. [ò-bí-n-nà] Father's domain;
lineage or clan.

Obinwa *nom phr* [ó-bì-nwá] A heart favourably disposed toward children.

Obinwanne *nom phr* [ó-bì-nwá-n-nē] Brotherly love or affection. Literally, heart (love) for siblings.

Obiọha *nom phr* [ó-bī-ò-hà], (*var*: **Obiọra** [ó-bī-ò-rà]) Literally, the heart of the community or clan, meaning a man who has the welfare of the people at heart. A benevolent philanthropist.

Obiọma *nom phr* (*var*: **Obioma(h)** [ó-bì-ó-má] A good (understand: kind, compassionate) heart. Also compassion or kindness.

Ọbụmnaeme *ut* [ó-bū-m-nà-è-mé]   I
am in charge here or I accept full
responsibility for what is going on.

Ọbụmselụ *int ut* [ò-bù-m-sè-lù]   Is it
my fault? Am I liable or responsible?

Ọchịagha *n* [ò-chí-ā-gh-ā]   Military
commander or general.

Ọdịnakachi   *ut*   [ó-dī-ná-ká-chī]
Committed into God's hand.

Ọdọemelam *sub ut* [ò-dó-é-mē-lām],
(*var*: **Ọzọemelam** [ò-zó-é-mē-lām],
Ọzọemela [ò-zó-é-mē-lā] or
Ọzọemena [ò-zó-é-mē-nā] May it
never happen again to me or enough is
enough.

Ọdụm *n* [ò-dú-m]   Lion.

Ọdụmegwu *nom phr* [ò-dù-mé-gwū] Awe-inspiring or dreadful lion.

Ọfọ *n* (*var*: **Ofor** or even **Offor**) [ò-fó] Divine retribution.

Ọfọegbu *ut* [ò-fó-é-gbū] Divine retribution or vengeance does not kill an innocent person.

Ọfọkansi *ut* [ò-fó-kā-n-sí] Divine retribution is more potent than witchcraft.

Ọgadịnma *ut* [ó-gā-dí-n-mā] Everything will be alright.

Ogbonna *nom phr* [ò-gbò-n-nā], (*var*: Ogbonnaya [ò-gbò-n-nā-yá]) Father's friend or pal; father's namesake.

148

Ogbuagụ *nom phr* [ò-gbú-ā-gʰū] A tiger killer. Also a title of nobility.

Ogbuehi *nom phr* [ò-gbú-ē-hī], (*var*: **Ogbuefi** [ò-gbú-ē-fī]) A cow killer. *Ogbuehi* is also a title of nobility.

Ogbuji *nom phr* [ò-gbú-jī] A yam plantation.

Oge(h) *n* [ó-gʰē]) God's time or timing.

Ogechi *nom phr* [ó-gʰē-chī], (*var*: **Ogechukwu** [ó-gʰē-chú-kwú) often abbreviated to **Oge(h)** above.

Ọgọbụnwanne *ut* [ó-gō-bū-nwá-n-nē] A person-in-law is a relative.

Ogu *n* [ó-gù] Uprightness, cleanness of hand, integrity or probity. Echeruo gives a metonymic definition of the word: "spike or wand (of wood or metal) symbolizing innocence and guiltlessness which is a piercing arrow for the guilty [...] The spike for innocence hurts only the guilty; "ogu" is thus the supreme emblem of guiltlessness" (122).

Oguama(lam) *imp ut* [ó-gù-á-mā-(lā-m)], (*var*: Oguama(nam) [ó-gù-á-mā-(nā-m)] May my uprightness and integrity preserve me, or may my uprightness and integrity never be called into question.

Ogubuike *ut* [ó-gù-bù-í-ké] Integrity and uprightness are a source of strength.

Ogubụnka *ut* [ó-gù-bú-n-ká]
Integrity and uprightness are a sure
path to long life.

Ogụgụa *n* [ò-gú-gū-á], (*var*: Ogụgụọ
[ò-gú-gū-á]) Comforter. Consoler. The
person who calms our fears.

Ogumka *ut* [ó-gūm-ká] I am of the
utmost uprightness, integrity, or
probity.

Ogwụdire *nom phr* [ó-gwú-dí-ì-rè]
Effective or efficacious medicine.

Ọhajụrụ *imp ut* [ò-hà-jú-rú] Let
everybody calm down.

Ọhaka(h) *ut* [ò-hà-ká], (*var*: Ọraka(h)
[ò-rà-ká] The community is preeminent.

151

Meaning: No one is greater than or above the community.

Ọhakwe *abr ut* [ò-hà-kwé]   If the people or the community agree or consent; or if the community permits.

Ọhale *abr ut* [ò-hà-lè-é]   I call the whole world to witness.

Ọhanụrụ *abr imp ut* [ò-hà-nù-rú] Let everyone hear.

Ọjị (*var:* Orjị) *n* [ó-jī]   Iroko tree. Just like *Osisiọma*, this name invokes the powerful imagery of a gigantic tree towering above all else, with roots firmly planted and reaching deep down into the ground.

Ojiakǫ (*var*: **Ojiakor**) *nom phr* [ò-jì-à-kó] Endowed with slyness or resourcefulness.

Ojike *nom phr* [ò-jì-í-ké] A person of tremendous strength, or endowed with power.

Ojinma *nom phr* [ò-jì-n-má] Endowed with beauty or an embodiment of beauty. Literally: he who possesses beauty.

Ǫjịnta (*var*: **Orjinta**) *nom phr* [ó-jì-n-tā] Little iroko tree. See *Ǫjị* above.

Okebugwu *ut* [ó-ké-bū-ù-gwù] A male child brings honour.

Okechi *nom phr* [ò-kè-é-chī], (*var*: **Okechukwu** [ò-kè-chú-kwú])

Gift from God.

Okeke *n* [ò-ké-kē], (*var*: **Okereke** [ò-ké-ré-kē]) A male child born on an **_Eke_** market day.

Okeọma *nom phr* [ò-kè-ó-má]   Good luck or fortune.

Okeosisi *nom phr* [ó-ké-ó-sí-sí], (*var*: **Okosisi** [ó-kó-sí-sí]) Great or male tree.

Okeugo) *nom phr* [ó-ké-ū-gʰō], (*var*: **Okugo** [ó-kú-gʰō]   Male eagle; could also mean great eagle.

Okezie *abr ut* [ó-kē-zí-é]   When the boundary acceptable to and respected by neighbours, it engenders good neighbourliness and peaceful coexistence.

Okorafọ *nom phr* [ò-kó-rá-fō], (*var*: **Okafọ** or **Okafor** [ò-ká-fō]) A male child born on the **Afọ** market day.

Okorie *nom phr* [ò-kó-rī-ē] A male child born on the **Orie** market day.

Okoro *n* [ò-kó-ró], (*var*: **Okolo** [ò-kó-ló] A male child; also a young man.

Okoroji *nom phr* [ò-kó-ró-jī] A young man rich in yams.

Okoroji *nom phr* [ò-kó-ró-jī] A young man whose majesty and magnificence are like those of the Iroko tree.

Okorojii *nom phr* [ò-kó-ró-ó-jí-ī] A black young man.

Okoronkwọ *nom phr* [ò-kó-ró-n-kwō] (*var*: **Okonkwọ** [ò-kó-n-kwō]) A male child born on the **Nkwọ** market day.

Ọkpankụ *nom phr* [ò-kpá-n-kú] The wood or log gatherer.

Okute or **Okuteh** *n* [ò-kú-tē], (*var*: **Okwute** [ò-kwú-tē]) Stone or rock. See the entry for *Nkume* in this section.

Okwu *n* [ó-kwú] Word. Also short form for the four names below.

Okwuchi *nom phr* [ó-kwú-chī], (*var*: **Okwuchukwu** [ó-kwú-chú- kwú] God's word, gospel or even sermon.

Okwudiri *sub ut* [ó-kwú-dī-rí], (*var*: **Okwudili** [ó-kwú-dī-lí]) May the word be fulfilled in the life of the person who uttered it.

Okwuọnụ *nom phr* [ó-kwú-ó-nū] Word of mouth.

Okwuorisa *nom phr* [ó-kw-ú-ò-rì-sà], (*var*: **Okwuolisa**) [ó-kw-ú-ò-lì-sà]) The word of God, same as *Okwuchi*.

Olehi *int ut* [ò-lé-hī], (*var*: **Oleshi** [ò-lé-shī]) When or what day? Also: when will it be?

Olekanma *int ut* [ò-lé-kā-n-mā] How much is enough?

Olisa(h) *n* [ò-lì-sà], (*var*: **Orisa(h)** [ò-rì-sà]) God. This is another name for *Chi*, *Chukwu* or *Chineke*.

Olisadebe(h) *ut* [ò-lì-sà-dè-bé] May God preserve.

Ọlụchi *nom* *phr* [ó-lú-chī], (*var*: **Ọlụchukwu** [ó-lú-chú-kwú]) God's handwork. God is seen as the architect of the young life.

Omenihu *nom phr* [ò-mé-ní-hú] An occurrence in accordance with one's fortune or destiny. This name also means "It happened during my time," meaning that the parents had given up all hope of having a child, or particularly a male child, and at the long last, their son was born.

Ọnụbụọgụ (*var*: Ọnụbọgụ) *ut* [ó-nú-bū-ò-gʰù]   The mouth is at the root of all conflict. There is an Igbo saying that the mouth is so quick to start a fight, but it is the hands that must carry the arms. The dangerous potential of the mouth setting the world ablaze with mere words is highlighted by the name *Ọnụbụọgụ* as a warning and reminder to all to weigh their words.

Ọnụegbu *ut* [ó-nú-é-gbū]   Words of mouth do not kill.

Ọnụkaọgụ *ut* [ó-nú-kā-ò-gʰù], (*var*: Ọnụkọgụ [ó-nú-kò-gʰù]) The mouth is more destructive than a raging war.

Ọnụma, (*var*: **Onumah**) *n* [ò-nù-mà] Sadness, rancour.

Ọnụnekwu(ruọha) *nom phr* [ó-nú-
ná-é-kwú(rú-ò-hà)], (*var:*
Ọnụnekwu(ruọra) [ó-nú-ná-é-
kwú(rú-ò-rà)] Spokesperson, champion,
or advocate for the community.

Ọnụnka, (*var:* **Onunkah**) *ut* [ó-nú-n-
kā]   The mouth never underestimates
its wants, wishes or worth.

Ọnụọha *nom phr* [ó-nú-ō-hā] (*var:*
Ọnụọra [ó-nú-ō-rā]) The community's
or clan's voice, mouthpiece or spokesperson.

Ọnwụ *n* [ó-nwú] Death. *Ọnwụ* is
often the short form of any of the longer
derivative names listed hereunder. It
also occurs as a stand-alone name as is
the case here. Why would parents give
this name to their son? Death has

challenged the philosophical imagination of the Igbo who see it as a thief, an impudent violator, a heartless deaf-and-dumb interlocutor and the ultimate evil. Yet no one can avoid having to deal with it. The following twelve names derived from Ọnwụ give us an insight into the cultural philosophy of the Igbo in regard of this phenomenon.

Ọnwụabụghenyi *ax ut* [ó-nwú-á-būgh-é-nyī], (*var*: Ọnwụabụenyi [ó-nwú-á-bū-é-nyī] Death is nobody's friend.

Ọnwụasọghanya *ax ut* [ó-nwú-á-sōgh-á-nyá], also Ọnwụasọanya [ó-nwú-á-sō-á-nyá] Death is impudent or insolent.

Ọnwụatụegwu *ax ut* [ó-nwú-á-tū-é-gwū], (Ọnwụatụghegwu [ó-nwú-á-tū-ghé-gwū] Death is fearless.

Ọnwụbiko *ut* [ó-nwú-bí-kō] Death, I (we) beg or appeal to you (to stop). This is a plea from a family that has had to deal with a number of deaths within a space of time before the birth of their male child. Just like *Amaefula* and *Ọzọemela*, *Ọnwụbiko* is a direct appeal to death to stop its deadly visit to the family.

Ọnwụdike *ut* i. [ó-nwú-dī-í-ké] Death is strong.

ii. [ó-nwú-dí-ké] The death of a great man.

Ọnwụegbu *abr ut* [ó-nwú-é-gbū], (*var*: Ọnwụegbuaha [ó-nwú-é-gbū-á-hà] Death cannot kill a name. As this name implies, the child who bears it was born after the death of some family member, possibly the father or grandfather whose lineage he will be continuing. A shout of victory, or at least a sigh of relief, *Ọnwụegbu* is also a consolatory boast that death has not succeeded in stamping out the family name.

Onwụegbuchulam *sub ut* [ó-nwú- é-gbū-chū-lām], (*var*: Egbuchulam [é-gbū-chū-lām]) May I not die an untimely death.

Ọnwụekwe *ut* [ó-nwú-é-kwē] Death does not entertain any dialogue.

Ọnwụeyi *abr ut* [ó-nwú-é-yī] Death does not schedule its visit.

Ọnwụka *abr ut* [ó-nwú-kā] (Short form of Ọnwụkanjọ [ó-nwú-kā-n-jó]) Death is the ultimate evil.

Ọnwụkwe *abr ut* [ó-nwú-kwé] If death permits me or spares my life.

Ọnwụmechiri *ut* [ó-nwú-mè-chì-rì], (*var*: Ọnwụmechili [ó-nwú-mè-chì-lì] Prevented by death.

Ọnwụmere *abr ut* [ó-nwú-m-ē-rē] Death is responsible, that is, death is the culprit. Death has a way of altering the course of family's life's journey. A male child born after a family experiences such a loss is likely to be given this name.

Ọnwụnma *abr ut* [ó-nwú-n-mā], (*var*: Ọnwụma [ó-nwú-mā]) Death knows when it will strike. Variously described as a thief, a heartless rodent and a hawk because of the sudden nature of its attack, death is notorious for not communicating its intentions to anyone.

Ọnwụsirike *ut* [ó-nwú-sī-rī-í-ké] Death is powerful.

Onyeabọ, (*var*: Onyeabọr) *abr ut* [ò-nyé-á-bō] Do not gloat over other people's misfortune or shortcoming. In Isiukwuatọ *Onyeabọ* also means "burden bearer" or the invisible helping hand.

Onyeaghala *imp ut* [ò-nyé-á-ghà-là] Let no one forget or forsake their kith and kin.

Onyeamalam *imp ut* [ò-nyé-á-mā-là-m] Let no one blame me.

Onyeańụla *imp ut* [ò-nyé-á-ṅù-là], (*var*: **Onyeańụna** [ò-nyé-á-ṅù-nà]) Let no one rejoice.

Onyebụchi *int ut* [ò-nyé-bú-chí], (*var*: **Onyewụchi** [ò-nyé-wú-chí] Who can claim to be God? This name is often shortened to *Bụchi*.

Onyebụnjọ *int ut* [ò-nyé-bú-n-jó] Who would claim to be an embodiment of evil?

Onyedịkachi *int ut* [ò-nyé-dī-kā-chí] Who can be compared or likened to God?

Onyedinma   *int ut*   [ò-nyé-dī-n-má]
Who is good? Who can claim goodness?

Onyekaba   *int ut*   [ò-nyé-ká-á-bá]
Who is the richest?

Onyekachi   *int ut*   [ò-nyé-ká-chí]
Who is greater than God?

Onyekaọdịrị *int ut* [ò-nyé-kā-ó-dì-rì],
(*var:* **Onyekaọdị** [ò-nyé-kā-ó-dì] Who
has it all made? Or, who is without
issues and problems?

Onyekwere   *int ut*   [ò-nyé-kwè-rè]
Who would have believed? This is one of
the names parents could give to their
son if, against all odds and after
exhausting all possible avenues to no
avail, they finally have a child.

Onyema *abr int ut* [ò-nyé-mā], (*var:*
Onyemaechi [ò-nyé-mā-é-chí]) Who

knows what tomorrow will bring? Also, who can foretell the future?

Onyemelam *imp ut* [ò-nyé-á-mā-là-m] Let no one blame, offend or provoke me.

Onyemso *ut* [ó-nyé-m-sò] The person who protects me (literally: the person I am following) is a warrior.

Onyenduzi *nom phr* [ó-nyé-n-dú-zí] A good leader or director.

Onyenso *int ut* [ò-nyé-n-sò], (*var* : **Onyeso** [ò-nyé-sò] Who is following or who is keeping pace? Meaning: who is next in line?

Onyenachi *nom phr* [ò-nyé-nā-chí] Short form of '*Onye na Chi ka ọha*' (One with God is greater in number than the crowd.)

Onyeukwu *nom phr* [ó-nyé-ú-kwú], (*var*: **Onyeuku** [ó-nyé-ú-kú] A great man.

Ọnyịaọha *nom phr* [ó-nyī-á-ò-hà] Confounding defiance for all and sundry.

Onyinye *n* [ò-nyì-nyé] Gift.

Onyinyechi *nom phr* [ò-nyì-nyé-chí], (*var*: **Onyinyechukwu** [ò-nyì-nyé-chú-kwú]) Gift from God.

Ọnyịrịmba *nom phr* [ò-nyì-rì-m-bā] He who defies a nation.

Ọpara(h) *n* [ó-pá-rá], (*var*: **Ọkpara**) [ó-kpá-rá] or **Ọkwara** [ó-kwá-rá]) The first son. As is the case in most traditional societies, the value, respect, and honour accorded the male Igbo child are utmost. It is even significantly more so in the case of the first son, who normally becomes the next head of the family, no matter his age, after the death of his father.

Ọparajiakụ *nom phr* [ó-pá-rá-jī-à-kù], (*var*: Ọkparajiakụ [ó-kpá-rá-jī-à-kù] A wealthy first son.

Ọpụrụm *abr ut* [ó-pū-rú-m], (*var*: Ọfụrụm [ó-fū-rú-m]) What worked for me might not work for everyone.

Ọrazulike *imp ut* [ò-rà-zù-lú-í-kē], (*var*: Ọhazuruike [ò-hà-zù-rú-í-kē]) Let everyone calm down. Like the name *Ọhajụrụ*, this name is used in suing for peace in the family, clan, or community.

Osimiri *n* [ò-sì-mì-rì] The sea, great river, ocean.

Osinachi *ut* [ó-sī-nā-chí]   Destiny. Literally, this name means 'It was predetermined or ordained by God.' The Igbo believe that one's destiny is written on the palm on his / her hand and this destiny is immutable. See *Chidera*.

Osisioma *nom phr* [ó-sí-sí-ó-má] Literally, a lovely tree, the name *Osisioma* is one of the few Igbo names that have the force of metaphorical evocation. The metaphor at work here is powerful: that of a great tree towering above all else, with its branches proudly spread out and roots reaching deep into the ground. When you imagine this imagery bathing in lush greenery with colourful flowers, then you get the clear picture of the majesty and magnificence this name is meant to conjure up in the minds of the Igbo.

Ọsọdịuru *nom phr* [ó-só-dī-ú-rū] A profitable race, meaning a worthy cause. The race or cause referred to in this name could include, but is not limited to, marriage, profession, or any other venture undertaken by the family. The name has a hint of gratitude to Providence for prospering the undertaking in question.

Ọsọndụ *nom phr* [ó-só-n-dʼū] A race or flight for refuge.

Osuji *n* [ò-sú-jī] A person consecrated to the yam deity.

Ọyịm *n* [ò-yì-m] My friend. Same name as *Enyim* or *Ogbo* (pronounced [ò-gbò-ó] Abịrịba, Ọhọfịa). Friendship in Igboland is a very strong bond, stronger most times than that between siblings, for as it is said in Igbo, you choose your friends, but have no control over who your siblings are.

Owuamalam *sub ut* [ó-wù-á-mā-lām], (also: **Owuamanam** [ó-wù-á-mā-lām] May I never be disgraced.

Oyirinna *nom phr* [ò-yì-rì-n-nà]   A son who resembles his father.

Ozioma(h) *nom phr*   [ó-zí-ó-má] Good news.

Ozodinihu *ut* [ò-zó-dī-ní-hú]   The future has in-built second chances. This hope in the great promise of the future governs Igbo optimism, and the name *Ozodinihu* simply means that as long as there is life, there is hope.

Ọzọemela *sub ut* [ò-zó-é-mē-lā],
(*var*: Ọdọemela [ò-dó-é-mē-lā] or
Ọzọemena [ò-zó-é-mē-nā])   May it
never happen again or may it stop
happening.

Ozurumba *nom phr*   [ò-zù-rù-m-bā]
Possessing a national reach or influence.

S / T

Sọpụrụchi *imp ut*   [só-pū-rú-chī],
(*var*: Sọpụrụchukwu   [só-pū-rú-chú-
kwú])   Have reverence for God.

Tobechi *imp ut* [tò-bé-chī], (*var*:
Tobechukwu [tò-bé-chú-kwú] Praise
God.

Toochi *imp ut* [tò-ó-chī], (*var*:
Toochukwu [tò-ó-chú-kwú]
Praise God.

U / Ụ

Ụbọchi *n* [ú-bò-chì]   Day, daylight.

Uche *n* [ú-chē]   Thought. Opinion.
Will. Judgment. Verdict. See the entry
for this name under the Girls' Names
section.

Uchechi *nom phr* [ú-chē-ē-chī] (*var:* **Uchechukwu** [ú-chē-chú-kwú]) God's opinion, will or verdict.

Uchefula *imp ut* [ú-chē-é-fù-là] Do not despair.

Uchendụ *nom phr* [ú-chē-n-ɗù] Thought or opinion about life.

Uchenna *nom phr* [ú-chē-n-nà] Father's thought, opinion, will or verdict.

Ude *n* [ù-dé] Ointment, cream, lotion, oil or fragrance.

Udeagha [ù-dé-á-ghā] Rumours of war.

Udechukwu *nom phr* [ù-dé-chū-kwū] God's fragrance.

Udo (*var:* **Udoh**) *n* [ù-ɗó] Peace.

Udochi *nom phr* [ù-ɗó-chī], (*var:* **Udochukwu** [ù-ɗó-chù-kwù]) God's peace, meaning peace *of*, *from* and/or *with* God.

Udodịrịm *sub ut* [ù-ɗó-dì-rí-m] May I have peace (of mind), or may peace be with me.

Udoka *ut* [ù-ɗó-kā] Peace is of paramount importance.

Ụdụnna *nom phr* [ú-ɗū-n-nā] Father's fame.

Ụfọmba *nom phr* [ù-fó-m-bà] The remnant of a people or clan.

Ụgbọ *n* [ú-gbó] A vehicle or vessel; cf. *ụgbọ-ala* (car), *ụgbọ-mmiri* (ship) and *ụgbọ-elu* (airplane).

Ụgbọaja *nom phr* [ú-gbó-à-jà] Vessel used for sacrifice.

Ụghaelumọ *ut* [ù-ghā-é-lū-n-mó-ọ]
(*var*: Ụghaerumọ [ù-ghā-é-rū-n-mó-
ọ]) You cannot lie to the spirits, deity
or the ancestors. Meaning: they cannot
be deceived.

Ugo *n* [ù-gʰò] The eagle. The majesty
of this king of birds is what is evoked in
this name from which longer names
derive as shown hereunder.

Ugoala *nom phr* [ù-gʰó-à-là] The
honour of the clan.

Ugochi *nom phr* [ù-gʰó-chí], (*var*:
Ugochukwu [ù-gʰó-chú-kwú])
God's honour and majesty.

Ugochinyere *nom phr* [ù-gʰò-chí-nyè-
rè] Honour bestowed by God.

Ugonna *nom phr* [ù-gʰò-n-nā]
Father's honour and majesty.

Ugoọjị *nom phr* [ù-gʰò-ó-jī], (*var:* Ugoọrjị or Ugorjị [ù-gʰó-jī]) The majesty of the iroko tree. See the entry for *Ojị*. The name *Ugoọjị* speaks to the majesty and magnificence of this giant tree.

Ugwu *n* i. [ù-gwù] Honour, respect or reverence.

ii. [ú-gwú] Hill or mountain.

Ugwueze *nom phr* [ù-gwù-é-zē] The honour of a king.

Ugwuka *abr ut* [ù-gwù-ká] Honour is supreme.

Ugwumba *nom phr* [ù-gwù-m-bā] The honour of a people, clan or nation.

Ugwunna *nom phr* [ù-gwù-n-nā] Father's honour.

Ugwunze *nom phr* [ù-gwú-n-zè] The honour of nobility.

Uju *n* [ù-jú] Abundance or affluence. See the entry under the name *Obianuju* in the Girls' Names section.

Ụka(h) *n* [ú-kā] Argument, dispute, misunderstanding; also: talk, discussion or conversation.

Ụkachukwu *nom phr* [ú-kā-chú-kwú] God's word or speech.

Ụkaegbu *abr ut* [ú-kā-égbū] Argument, dispute or conversation does not kill a relationship.

Ụkaibe *nom phr* [ú-kā-í-bʲē] Public opinion.

Ụkanwa *nom phr* [ú-kā-n-nwá], (*var*: **Ụkanwanta** [ú-kā-n-nwá] The ordeal of having a child. Some parents experience great tribulations associated with child-bearing: miscarriages, still births, sudden death syndrome, or even barrenness, etc. The name *Ụkanwa* for them, summarizes the distress they have been through before the arrival of their child. The name also means: for the sake of the child. In this case, one of the parents (usually the father) decides to forgive the spouse and continue with the marriage in spite of a grievous offence, *for the child's sake.*

Ụkaọha *nom phr* [ú-kā-ò-hà], (*var*: Ụkọha [ú-kō-hà]) Public conversation, debate or opinion. Also, the talk of the town.

Ụkaọma *nom phr* [ú-kā-ó-má], (*var*: Ụkọma [ú-kō-má]) Good word or conversation; also good report.

Ụkaọnụ *nom phr* [ú-kā-ó-nū], (*var:* Ụkọnụ [ú-kó-nū]) Word of mouth or argument.

Ụkaụzọ *nom phr* (*var:* Ukauzor) [ú-kā-ú-zō] Journey conversation.

Ụkazụ *nom phr* [ú-kā-á-zú] Gossip.

Ụkpabị *n* [ù-kpá-bī] "Name for God, or Supreme Being" (Echeruo, 165).

Ụkwụ *n* [ú-kwú] Foot or leg.

Ụlụ *n* [ùlú] Second son of the mother.

Ume(h) *n* [ù-mé] "A person associated with a cult; a cult slave" (Echeruo, 160).

Umezuruike *imp ut* [ù-mé-zù-rú-í-kē] Let afflictions cease.

Uruakpa *abr ut* [ù-rú-á-kpā] A wealthy man is never dishonoured or held in derision.

Ụwà (*var*: Uwah) *n* [ù-wà] The world. *Ụwa* also refers to destiny, fate or providence in the sense that providence governs the affairs of the world. It could also be used metonymically to refer to people that make up the world. Each person has their personal space or **ụwa**, their destiny in the Igbo cosmos, the unfolding of which is governed by providence; in this sense, **ụwa** refers to life as it is experienced by the individual.

Ụwadịegwu *ax ut* [ù-wà-dì-é-gwū] The world is full of mysteries or wonders. The incomprehensibility of some phenomena around us has boggled the minds of the brightest of Igbo thinkers over the centuries. The unsolved mysteries of life are an indicator in Igbo philosophical thought of a superior intelligence that governs the unfolding of events beyond human comprehension and control. *Ụwadịegwu* is an expression of this epistemological reality.

Ụwaezighozi *ax ut* [ù-wà-é-zì-ghì-ó-zí] Destiny does not communicate its unfolding or intentions.

Ụwakwe *abr ut* [ù-wà-kwé] If the world, destiny or life permits.

Ụwanna *nom phr* [ù-wà-n-nā] Father's world or destiny.

Ụwaọma *nom phr* [ù-wà-ó-má] Good fortune or luck. Literally: good world.

Ụwazie *abr ut* [ù-wà-zí-é] In an ideal world, or by dint of good fortune.

Ụwazuruike *imp ut* [ù-wà-zù-rú-í-kē]   Let everyone calm down or bury the hatchet.

Ụzọ (*var*: Uzo(r)) *n* [ú-zō]   The way or road.

Ụzọamaka *ut* [ú-zō-à-má-ká]   The road, or way (or journey) is most beautiful.

Ụzọanya *nom phr* [ú-zō-á-nyā]   A long distance journey.

Ụzọchi *nom phr* [ú-zō-chī], (*var*: Ụzọchukwu [ú-zō-chú-kwú])   God's or godly ways or means.

Ụzọdịnma *nom phr* [ú-zō-dí-n-mā] A good road or journey. See the entry for this name in the Girls' Names section.

Ụzọgọ (*var:* **Uzogo(r)**) *nom phr* [ú-zō-ó-gō] The road or journey to the family-in-law.

Ụzọha *nom phr* [ú-zō-ò-hà] The road or way taken by all.

Ụzọhọ *nom phr* [ú-zō-ó-hó-ō] (*var:* **Ụzọhụrụ** [ú-zō-ó-hú-rū]) A new way or road.

Ụzọije *nom phr* [ú-zō-í-jē] Journey or mission.

Ụzọma *nom phr* [ú-zō-ó-má] A good journey. See the entry for this name under the Girls' Name section.

Ụzọndu *nom phr* [ú-zō-n-dʰū] The way of life, also the way to life.

Ụzọnna *nom phr* [ú-zō-n-nā] Father's trajectory or path. This name also implies the figurative use of the word *path*, meaning destiny.

Ụzọukwu *nom phr* [ú-zō-ú-kwú]   The great or superior way; also the highway.

Z

Zereibe *imp ut* [zè-ré-í-bʲ ē], (*var*: Zeribe) [zè-rí-bʲ ē]   Deal cautiously with people.

Zimakọ(r) *abr imp ut*   [zí-mā-kō], (*var*: Ibezimakọ(r)   [í-bʲ ē-zí-mā-kō] Teach or show me some deftness or cleverness. This is an open challenge to the general public to demonstrate some adroitness.

PART TWO
GIRLS' NAMES

A

Ada *n* [à-dɑ̀ á] *Ada* is the name generally given to the first daughter of the family, and means exactly that: the first daughter. Daughters are so precious in the Igbo society, not only because of the honour and wealth they add to the family upon their marriage (through bride price), but especially because they are the link to the greater-family. They are, therefore, groomed to be exemplary, true representatives; ambassadresses, if you will, of their families. As a result, the first daughter, wields a lot of power and authority in her family, after the first son. Important family decisions and actions cannot be taken in the absence of the first-born daughter. Her younger sisters look up to her and she is expected to set a positive tone for the family's female ethic, morality and industry. First daughters often assume the role of mothers toward their younger siblings as early as the pre-teen years, and all through their adult lives. Thus the name *Ada* carries with it immense expectations, honour and responsibility.

Adaeze *nom phr* [à-ɗá-é-zē] Princess. *Adaeze* literally means the first daughter of the king. Note that the Igbo do not have royal families (see Afigbo, 484–487), meaning that royalty and chieftaincy are not hereditary, but are conferred on merit to deserving men and women who have distinguished themselves in service to their communities. The Igbo society being more or less an egalitarian society, there is the saying that everyman is a king in his own household. Thus the name *Adaeze* is not a royal title, but speaks to the parents' yearnings for future greatness for their daughter.

Adakụ *nom phr* [à-ɗá-à-kù] The daughter who brings wealth. As indicated in the name *Ada*, to which is added the suffix *àkù* (wealth), through the customary practice of bride price, daughters are a source of wealth for their families, especially if their husbands are rich. Marriage in Igboland, as in many

African societies, is not just a union between husband and wife, but between their two families and their extended arms. As a result, the husband is expected to assume financial and general welfare responsibilities of his wife's family. The lot of any family is generally expected to improve with the marriage of their daughter. *Adaku* is thus an aspirational name that speaks to the parents' yearnings for an upward mobility and a greater tomorrow at the birth of their daughter.

Adanma *nom phr* [à-ɗá-n-mā] The daughter who epitomizes beauty. The concept of beauty in the Igbo society encompasses physical attributes and extends much more than skin-deep to include one's attitudes, dispositions toward others and general comportment. *Adanma* therefore refers to a daughter who embodies feminine graces and humanness.

Adanna *nom phr* [à-ɗá-n-nà] Beloved of her father. *Adanna* means much more than Daddy's girl. It speaks of a daughter who is favoured by her father. More often than not, this name is given to a daughter who has a strikingly close resemblance to her father. In addition, *Adanna* refers to the close affection between father and daughter, which normally confers on her special authority that other daughters do not have. After all, she is the first daughter!

Adanne *nom phr* [à-ɗá-n-nē], (*var:* **Adane** [à-ɗá-nē])   Beloved of her mother. All that is said above about *Adanna* equally applies to *Adanne* with the only difference that they obtain between the daughter and her mother.

Adanze *nom phr*   [à-ɗá-n-zè]   *Nze* is a chieftaincy title. *Adanze* is almost an identical name to *Adaeze* above. It means the first daughter of a chief or nobleman. All that is said about *Adaeze* equally applies to *Adanze*.

Adaobi *nom phr*   [à-ɗá-ō-bī]   The first daughter of the family or household. So, what is the difference between *Ada* and *Adaobi*? In a polygamous family, there may be more than two or more first daughters, depending of the number of wives in the family. *Adaobi*, being the very first daughter of the household, is therefore first among equals (the other first daughters). She receives her birthright before the others and enjoys greater authority than them.

Adaọma *nom phr* [à-dá-ó-má]   A beautiful daughter. Everything said about *Adanma* applies to this name.

Adaugo *nom phr* [à-dá-ù-gò]   A daughter of distinction. *Ugo* literally means *eagle*, and just as the eagle is the king of birds, this daughter is customarily thought to be endowed with supremacy over all of her siblings.

Adịmụkọ *ut* [á-dìm-ù-kó]   An expression of pride and self-worth, this name literally means "I am priceless" or "I am unique." It is normally given by parents who either found it difficult to have a child at all, or have had all male children before the arrival of their daughter. In either case, the name speaks to the invaluable worth of their daughter.

Akachi *nom phr* [á-ká-chī] God's hand. See the entry for this name in the Boys' Names section.

Akụdo *nom phr* [à-kú-ū-ḍ ō] Liter-ally, peaceful riches. This name refers to wealth gotten through honest means. See the explanation for this name in the Boys' Names section.

Akụnna *nom phr* [à-kù-n-nà] Father's wealth. As in the name *Adaku*, *Akụnna* has in view the father's wealth laid aside for the daughter to enjoy later in life. It can also refer to the parents' hope of their daughter being a source of wealth for the family.

Akụọma *nom phr* [à-kù-ó-má] Good wealth, meaning wealth gotten through transparently legitimate means. As in *Akụdo* above, this name underlines the premium traditional Igbo society placed on integrity, societal ethics and morality.

Alaọma *nom phr* [à-là-ó-má] Literally, good land. But *Alaọma* refers to the clan and underlines the sterling qualities of the parents' clan, either the father's or the mother's, but in most cases, the latter.

Ama(h) *n* [á-má] *Ama* refers to family, household or clan. The name celebrates the family unit as indivisible and central to life. It also speaks to the Igbo philosophy that places communal life above that of the individual, the nucleus of which is the family.

Amaefule *imp ut* [á-má-é-fū-lē], (*var:* **Amaefula** [á-má-é-fū-lā]) May the family or clan endure. *Amaefule* is normally given to a child, boy or girl, born into a family that has experienced series of tragic events. It is thus a prayer that the family be spared any further occurrence of tragedy so there could be posterity.

Amaka *abr ut* [à-má-ká]   *Amaka* is the
shortened form of *Nwamaka* [nwá-á-má-ká]
A child who is the epitome of beauty. See this
name in the Boys' Names section.

Amarachi *nom phr* [à-mà-rá-chī]   God's
Grace.

Anayọ *abr imp ut* [á-ná-ā-yó], (*var:* **Kanayọ**
([kà-á-ná-ā-yó])   Let's keep praying. This
name could be given for a number of reasons,
including, but not limited to, a couple has been
praying for a son, but had a baby-girl instead;
or the couple had experienced the death of an
infant child or more, and are praying that their
daughter will live and not die; it could also be
that the mother experienced some difficulty
during pregnancy or at the birth of her child
and the prayer is for the mother's survival. The
name could also be given to a baby-girl whose
grand-parents – paternal or maternal – have
been experiencing some life's challenges.

Aṅụrị *n* [á-ṅū-rí]   Joy.

CH

Chetachi *imp ut* [chè-tá-chī], (*var*: **Chetachukwu** [chè-tá-chū-kwū]) *Cheta-chi* is an exhortation, not so much of the child as of the society, to remember God who has shown Himself mighty in the lives of the parents by giving them a child. This name is an expression of gratitude to God for His favor. Together with the next two names, *Chetachi* is normally abbreviated to *Cheta*.

Chetanna *imp ut* [chè-tá-n-nā]   Remember your father, meaning do not take your father for granted. Children are expected, as soon as they get established in life, to take care of, and provide for their parents especially in their parents' old age.

Chetanne *imp ut* [chè-tá-n-nē]   Remember your mother. Everything said about the father above applies equally to the mother.

Chialụka *ut* [chí-á-lú-ká], (*var*: Alụka   [à-lú-ká])   God has done a marvelous work. The birth of a child provides the parents the opportunity to express their gratitude to God for seeing them through life-and-death circumstances and situations. *Chialụka* celebrates God's intervention in their family life in ways that exceeds all their expectations.

Chiamaka   *ut*   [chí-ā-mā-kā]   (*var*: **Chukwuamaka** [chú-kwú-ā-mā-kā])   God is Excellent. The excellency of God is central to Igbo religious philosophy. He demonstrates this excellency in His just reward: good for the upright and evil for the wicked. The birth of a child is seen as one of His acts of reward and *Chiamaka* is a grateful affirmation of this divine attribute.

Chiamara *nom phr* [chí-à-mà-rà]   God of grace. Parents who have been beneficiaries of God's grace and favor exclaim here the name of their God with regard to this specific attribute. While the emphasis is on grace in *Amarachi*, the focus in *Chiamara* is on God.

Chibuike *ut* [chí-bū-ī-kē]   God is the source of strength.

Chibudo *ut* [chí-bū-ūdⁱ ó]   God is peace. Inter- and intra-family disputes are constant staples in the Igbo family dynamics. If in the midst of strife and, sometimes, outright hostility, a child is born, the parents are presented with the opportunity to dream of a better future. By giving their daughter the name *Chibudo*, the parents are suing for peace, urging the warring factions to seek peace which God can broker.

Chibuzo *ut* [chí-bū-ūzō]   God is first, meaning God is pre-eminent. Pronounced this way, *Chibuzo* literally means *God comes first*.

When it is pronounced as [chí-bù-zō], it means God is the way. In either case, this name, given to boys and girls alike, expresses the Igbo belief in the pre-eminence of God.

Chichetara(m) *ut* [chí-chè-tā-rā(m)]   God remembered (me). This name is given by parents who have tried everything possible to have a child and have not been successful, or had their child much later than their peers. It is an acknowledgement of God's faithfulness to them.

Chidị *abr ut* [chí-dì], (also: **Chukwudị** [chú-kwú-dī])   There is God. See the entry for this name in the Boys' Names section. *Chidị* means *God is*, and is completed by whatever attribute of God that follows it, as in the next six entries.

Chidịebere *ut* [chí-dì-è-bé-rē]   God is merciful.

Chidike *ut* [chí-dì-í-ké]   God is powerful.

Chidịndụ *ut* [chí-dì-n-d̶ū]   God is alive.

Chidịnma *ut* [chí-dì-n-má]   God is good.

Chidịnso *ut* [chí-dì-n-só]   God is near. This name is basically the same as *Chinọnso*.

Chidịnsọ *ut* [chí-dī-n-só]   God is holy.

Chidozie *ut* [chí-d̶ō-zí-é]   May God protect or preserve.

Chiedozie *ut* [chí-é-d̶ó-zí-é]   God has preserved.

Chiemela *ut* [chí-é-méé-lá]   Thank God. Literally, God has done well. This name is an expression of gratitude to God for all He has done in the lives of the family members, especially for giving them a child.

Chiemezie *ut* [chí-é-mē-zí-é]   God has perfected.

Chiemezuo   *ut*   [chí-é-mé-zū-ó], (*var*: **Chiemezue**   [chí-é-mé- ū-zé])   God has fulfilled His promise.

Chigọzie *imp ut* [chí-gō-zí-é]   May God bless.

Chigọziri(m) *ut* [chí-gō-zī-rī(m)], (*var*: **Chigọzili(m)**   [chí-gō-zī-rī(m)]   (I am) Blessed by God.

Chika *abr ut* [chí-kā]   God is supreme or preeminent.

Chikaọdịrị *ut* [chí-kā-ó-dì-rì], (*var*: **Chikaọdịlị** [chí-kā-ó-dì-lì]   God is sovereign. It is all up to God to decide or God has the final say.

Chike *abr ut* [chí-kēé]   As long as one is created by God, one's destiny is secure. This name has the same meaning as *Chidera*; (*var*: [chí-ké] which is the short form of *Chibuike*.)

Chikezie *ut* [chí-kē-zí-é]   Whatever God has made or created is perfect and cannot be improved upon.

Chikwe(m) a*br ut* [chí-kwé(m)]   If God permits (me) or God being on my side. As much as the Igbo believe strongly in industry and hard-work, they also believe in destiny and providence. In other words, hard work alone does not guarantee success in life. They strongly believe that for a person to be successful, God has to crown his or her efforts and industry with success. Many a hardworking person is known to struggle to make ends meet, and *Chikwe(m)* is an indirect appeal to God for leniency and help based on this philosophy.

Chikwesịrị *ut* [chí-kwè-sì-rì], (*var*: **Chikwesịlị** [chí-kwè-sì-lì])   God is worthy. Each bearer of this name normally completes the meaning how they see fit. The most common are God is worthy of praise, honour, glory, trust, etc.

Chima *abr ut*   [chí-mā], (*var*: **Chukwu-ma(h)** [chú-kwú-mā])   God knows. See the Igbo belief in the perfect knowledge of God expressed by this name in the Boys Names' section.

Chimezie *imp ut* [chí-mē-zí-é], (*var*: **Mezie** [mē-zi-é])   May God make perfect.

Chinaecherem *ut*   [chí-nā-é-chē-rém] God thinks about or for me. One of the many Igbo names that demonstrate reliance on God for virtually all of life's existential challenges, *Chinaecherem* celebrates God as an incomparable, trustworthy ally.

Chinaemerem *ut* [chí-nā-é-mē-rém], (*var*: **Chinemerem**) [chí-né-mē-rém],   God acts on my behalf. This is another name that expresses reliance on God.

Chinaenye *ut* [chí-nā-è-nyé], (*var:* **Chinenye** [chí-nē-nyé] or **Chukwunenye** [chú-kwú-nē-nyé]) God provides. The notion of God's provision for his creatures is strongly entrenched in Igbo philosophy. The Igbo gratefully recognize that everything they own comes from God as a special provision. As it was pointed out in the name *Chikwem*, this hard-held belief does not interfere with the Igbo work ethic and industry.

Chinasa *ut* [chí-nà-á-sā] God answers (on my behalf). This deference to God as the spokesperson is typical of the Igbo who normally appeal to divine alliance and intervention, especially when faced with intractable existential threats or all-powerful adversaries. This name is a self-effacing response of parents who recognize their cause to be just and thus appeal to the all-knowing God to adjudicate on their behalf.

Chinaza *abr ut* [chí-nā-à-zá] God answers (prayers). This acknowledgement that God not only hears, but answers the prayers of those who believe in Him, is a direct expression of gratitude to God for His love and involvement in their lives. The parents whose daughter is named *Chinaza*, might have prayed specifically for a daughter, or generally for a child; or it could be they had prayed for deliverance from another existential situation in which God intervened.

Chinedu(m) *ut* [chí-nā-ē-dú(m)] God is the (my) guide or leader. The journey through the rugged and dangerous terrains of life requires the leading of an all-knowing guide who is competent and strong enough to safely guide through this earthly journey.

Chinenye *abr ut* [chí-nē-nyé], (*var:* Chukwunenye) [chú-kwú- nē-nyé] God is the giver. This is a shortened form of *Chinenyendu*, God is the giver of life. Igbo religious philosophy is definite and unanimous in attributing life and human existence to God. Indeed, every Igbo acknowledges owing not only their life, but everything they possess to divine providence. *Chinenye* gives expression to this religious belief.

Chineso *ut* [chí-nē-sò]   God keeps (me or us) company.

Chinọnso *ut*   [chí-nō-n-só], (*var*: **Chukwu-nọnso**) [chú-kwú-nō-n-só])   God is ever near. The belief in a personal God creates a sense of proximity, even intimacy between the Igbo and their God.

Chinọnye *sub ut* [chí-nō-nyé], (*var*: **Chukwunọnye** [chú-kwú-nō-nyé]) May God be (abide) with (me or us)

Chinwe *abr ut* [chí-nwē]   Belonging or belongs to God. Usually the short form of longer names as in the next six entries.

Chinweakụ *ut* [chí-nwē-à-kù]   Wealth belongs to (or comes from) God.

Chinweike *ut*   [chí-nwē-í-ké]   Power belongs to God.

Chinweikpe   *ut*   [chí-nwé-í-kpé] Judgment belongs to God.

Chinwendụ *ut* [chí-nwē-n-dᵇ ù]   Life belongs to God or God is the source of life. See Chinenye above. *Chinwendụ* particularly expresses God's ownership of life, especially in the sense that this life is protectively hidden away in God. This name is therefore a declaration of the divine security enjoyed by the Igbo.

Chinweụba *ut* [chí-nwē-ūbá]   Wealth belongs to God, meaning that wealth comes from God.

Chinyere abr *ut* [chí-nyè-rè], (also:
Chukwunyere [chú-kwú-nyè-rè]) Endowed
by God.

Chinyereze *ut* [chí-nyē-rē-é-zē] Royalty or
kingship is bestowed by God; in other words, a
king is God-ordained.

Chioma *nom phr* [chí-ó-má] Good God,
good fortune or good providence. *Chioma* is a
celebration of God's goodness toward His
creation.

Chisom *ut* [chí-sōm], (*var:* **Chukwusom**)
[chú-kwú-sōm] God is with me, or God is on
my side. No adversary can be so formidable as
to withstand God. So when Igbo parents
declare that God is on their side, the
implication is that they are invincible. By giving
their daughter this name, the parents are
boasting of the unfailing quality of divine
protection.

Chizara(m) *ut* [chí-zā-rā-(m)]   God answered me (my prayers).

Chukwudị *ut* [chú-kwú-dī]   God is or there is God (See **Chidị** above).

E

Ebere *n* [è-bé-rē]   Mercy, kindness and compassion.

Eberechi *nom phr* [è-bé-rē-chī], (*var*: **Eberechukwu** [è-bé-rē-chú-kwú])   God's mercy, kindness and compassion.

Ebube *n* [è-bù-bè]   Glory, wonder or miracle.

Ebubechi *nom phr* [è-bù-bé-chī] (*var*: **Ebubechukwu** [è-bù-bé-chū-kwū])   God's glory or miracle.

Echefula *imp ut* [é-chē-fū-lā], (*var*:
Echefulachi [é-chē-fù-là-chí] Do not forget
God.

Ejitụ *abr ut* [é-jì-tú]   To be held in trust
temporarily. Such was the high infant mortality
rate in those days that babies were not
expected to survive onto their first birthday.
Hence the name *Ejitụ*, which literally means:
let's hold him or her in our hands for a while.
Parents who have repeatedly had this
experience were more likely to give this name
to their newborn, which smacks of resignation
to fate.

Ekenma *nom phr* [è-ké-n-mā]   The beauty
associated with **Eke** market day. This means
that the beautiful baby-girl who bears this
name was born on an **Eke** day. For the parents
who choose this name, the **Eke** market day has
become the very definition of feminine beauty.

Ekeọma *nom phr*   i. [è-ké-ó-má]   Good
Eke market day.

ii. [è-kè-ó-má]   Good or favourable fate or destiny.

Elewachi *imp ut* [é-lé-wá-chī]   Let's wait and see what God will do.

Emezue *abr ut* [é-mé-zū-é] (*var*: **Emezuo**) [é-mé-zū-ó])   When one fulfills one's promise, there is the sense of accomplishment. Promise-keeping is of paramount importance in Igbo interpersonal dynamics. This ideal is so prized that beloved civic leaders are sometimes fondly called '*Ọ kaa, O mee*': a man of his words.

Enyịoma *nom phr* [é-nyī-ó-má]   Good friend.

Erinma *abr ut* [è-rí-n-mā]   If beauty were edible! One of the names the Igbo use to eulogize beauty in their daughters, *Erinma* is reserved for extremely beautiful girls.

Ezenwanyị *nom phr* [é-zē-nwá-nyī]
Queen. See the name *Adaeze* for commentary
on royalty and kingship.

Ezinma *nom phr* [é-zí-n-mā]   Beauty in its
very essence.

Ezinne *nom phr* [é-zí-n-nē]   Beloved
mother.

Ezinwa *nom phr*   [é-zí-nwā]   Precious
child.

Ezinwanne *nom phr* [é-zí-nwá-n-nē]
Precious sibling, in this case, sister, or also
precious daughter of her mother's.

Ezịọma *nom phr* [è-zí-ó-má]   Good family.
Just like Alaọma, *Ezịọma* is the parents'
expression of pride in their family.

Eziuche *nom phr* [é-zí-ú-chē]   Good
opinion, will, thought or verdict.

I / Ị / K / M

Ifeyinwa *ut* [í-fé-é-yī-nwā]   There is nothing is as precious as a child. As is the case in societies everywhere, the child is the future of the society. The preciousness of the Igbo child and the society's hope of a better future are better understood by the way the extended family overly pampers the child. It is not uncommon for each adult member of the family to give the child a name of their own choosing, that reflects both their admiration of and aspiration for this child. This generosity in naming the child is often matched with a generosity in gift-giving to and care of the child as family members vie to out-give one another.

Ihechi *n* [ì-hé-chī]   Divine light.

Ihechiḷụrụ(m) *nom phr* [í-hé-chí-lū-rū(m)] What God did (for me), or God did me a favour.

Ihechimere *nom phr* [í-hé-chí-mērē]
God's handiwork. Also God's favor.

Iheoma *nom phr* [í-hé-ó-má], (*var*: **Ifeoma**
[í-fé-ó-má]) Good news.

Iheukwu(mere) *ut* [í-hé-ú-kwú(mere)]
Great news or occurrence (broke); or
something great happened.

Ịhụnanya *n* [í-hū-nā-á-nyá] Love.

Ịhụnayachi *nom phr* [í-hū-nā-á-nyá-chī],
(*var*: **Ịhụnayachukwu**) [í-hū-nā-á-nyá-chū-
kwū] God's love.

Ihuọma *nom phr* [í-hú-ó-má], (*var*:
Iruọma [í-rú-ó-má] or **Ivuọma** [í-vú-ó-má])
Good luck, or good fortune.

Ijendụ *nom phr* [í-jē-n-dʲū] Life's journey.

Ijeọma *nom phr* [í-jē-ó-má]   Good journey.
The journey referred to here is generally that of
marriage. The couple each took a journey,
literally, toward each other: the man to his
bride's hometown, and the bride to her groom's
home. When the marriage is blessed with a
child, the couple has the opportunity to declare
their journey a blessing and a success, *Ijeọma*.
This name is also given to a child born when
her mother or parents were on their way to
somewhere.

Izu *n* [ì-zù]   Wisdom.

Izuchi *nom phr* [ì-zú-chī], (*var*:
Izuchukwu [ì-zù-chú-kwú]) God's wisdom.

Kanayọ *imp ut* [kà-á-ná-ā-yó]   Let's keep
praying. See *Anayọ*.

Kaọsọrọchi *abr ut* [kà-ó-sō-rō-chí], (*var*:
Kọsọrọchi [kò-ó-sō-rō-chí]) Literally: As it
pleases God; meaning: May God's will be done.

217

Kelechi *imp ut* [kè-lé-chī], (*var:*
Kelechukwu [kè-lé-chú-kwú]) Give thanks
to God, or thanks be to God.

Mezie *abr ut* [mè-zí-é] (*var:* **Chimezie**
above) May God make perfect.

Mgbechi *nom phr* [m-gbé-chī] God's time
or timing. This name means exactly the same
thing as *Ogechi* hereunder.

Mgbeọdịchinma *nom phr* [m-gbé-ó-dī-chīn-mā] God's time is the best, (literally:
whenever it pleases God.)

N

Nchekwube *n* [n-chē-kwú-bú] Great
expectation, hope or trust. It goes without
saying that the parents who give this name to
their child are, through it, praying for and
prophesying a great future for him or her.

Ndidi *n* [n-dì-dì]   Patience or endurance. The Igbo believe this virtue conquers all things and are quick to urge and prescribe patience to anyone who is facing a trying situation.

Ndubuaku *ut*   [n-dù-bú-à-kù]   Life is wealth.

Ndukaku *ut* [n-dū-ká-à-kù]   Life is worth more than riches

Ngozi *n* [n-gó-zí]   Blessing.

Ngozichi *nom phr* [n-gó-zí-chī] (*var*: **Ngozichukwu** [n-gó-zí-chú-kwú])   God's blessing.

Ngozika *abr ut* [n-gó-zí-kā]   Blessing is of paramount importance.

Njideaka *nom phr*   [n-jì-dᵖ é-á-kā] Assurance and confidence. *Njideaka* literally refers to 'having a firm grip on something'.

Njideka *ut* [n-jì-ɖé-kā]   There is a more abiding assurance in ownership than in pursuit. This name roughly translates the axiomatic expression 'a bird in hand is worth two in the bush' and is analogous to *Nkemjika* below.

Nkechi *abr* *ut*   [n-kè-chí], (*var*: **Nkechinyere** [n-kè-chí-nyē-rē]) Whatever God has given. This philosophical name means that you don't get to choose your child – boy or girl. You receive with gratitude whichever God in His mercy gives you, especially in a family that has had a couple of daughters and had been praying for a son.

Nkeiru(ka) *ut* [n-kè-í-rū(-kā)]   The future (understand posterity) is greater. The future greatness of a family is always projected on the children, especially on the daughter (see *Adakụ* above).

Nkem *pos pron* [n-kém]   Mine or my own.
Often the shortened form of the next three
names of which it is the prefix.

Nkemakọlam *sub ut*   [n-kè-m-á-kō-lām])
May my share always belong to me, or be there
for me.

Nkemdịrịm *sub ut*   [n-kè-m-dì-rí-m], (*var:*
Nkemdịlịm [n-kè-m-dì-lí-m]   May what is
mine always be mine.

Nkemka *abr ut*   [n-kè-m-kā], (*var:*
Nkemjika [n-kè-m-jī-ká])   I have the best
part or share. What I have is of greater value.

Nkeonyere *abr ut*   [n-kè-ó-nyè-rè]
Whatever gift He (God) gives is perfect.

Nkwachi(kwere) *nom phr* [n-kwā-chí(kwē-
rē)]   God's promise.

Nnamụrụ *nom phr* [n-nā-mù-rù]   Her
father's child.

Nneamaka *ut* [n-né-ā-mā-kā]   Mother is the epitome of beauty.

Nnealọ *ut* [n-né-ā-lō], (*var*: Nneayọ [n-né-ā-yō])   Mother has returned. This is one of the names the Igbo use in expressing the reincarnation of a family member, in this case, the mother.

Nneka *ut* [n-né-kā]   Mother is supreme.

Nnenna *nom phr*   [n-né-n-nā]   Paternal grandmother. Like *Nnealọ*, *Nnenna* is given to a baby girl who has a striking resemblance to or is believed to be the reincarnation of a deceased family member. It refers to the reincarnation of the paternal or maternal grandmother.

Nnenne *nom phr*   [n-né-n-né]   Maternal grandmother. As stated in *Nnenna* and *Nneayọ* above, parents who give this name to their daughter believe her to be the reincarnation of her grandmother.

Nneọma *nom phr* [n-né-ó-má]   Good mother.

Nnezi *nom phr* [n-né-ē-zī]   Mother of the clan or household.

Nọnyerem *imp ut* [nō-nyé-rém]   Abide with me or keep me company.

Nwada(h) *n* [nwá-ā-ɗ ā]   Miss (as in the title Miss Universe or Miss Jones.) Though a title, *Nwada* is also given to girls as a first name. See *Ada*.

Nwadịnma *nom phr* [nwá-dī-n-mà] Precious child.

Nwadịụtọ *nom phr* [nwá-dī-ū-tó]   Sweet, that is darling, child.

Nwakaego *ut* [nwá-kā-ē-g̊ō]   A child is more precious than money.

Nwakakụ *ut* [nwá-ká-ā-kū]   A child is worth more than wealth.

Nwakanma *ut* [nwá-kā-n-má]   A child is priceless. This name also means: I would rather have a child or a child is of the greatest value.

Nwamaka *ut* [nwá-ā-mā-kā]   A child who is the epitome of beauty. See the name *Amaka* above.

Nwanganga *nom phr* [nwá-n-gà-n-gà]   A child who is the source of pride.

Nwanyịeze *nom phr* [nwá-nyī-é-zē]   A girl of royal extraction.

Nwanyịnma *nom phr* [nwá-nyī-n-mā]   A girl who is the epitome of beauty.

Nwanyịoma *nom phr* [nwá-nyī-ó-má] A beautiful girl.

Nwaụlọ *nom phr* [nwá-ú-lò] Homely child.

O / Ọ

Obenwa *nom phr* [ó-bé-nwā], (*var:* **Oberenwa** [ó-bé-ré-nwā]) A little child (*little* in the affective sense).

Ọbịanuju *nom phr* [ọ-bị-á-nū-jú] She who comes (is born) in the season of plenty, meaning 'born into affluence.'

Obioma *nom phr* [ó-bī-ó-má] A loving heart.

Ọdịnachi *ut* [ó-dī-nā-chí] God is sovereign or it all depends on destiny.

Ọdịnakachi *ut* [ó-dī-ná-ká-chī]
Committed into God's hand.

Ọgadịnma *ut* [ọ-gā-dí-n-mā]   Everything
will be alright or all will be well.

Oge *n* [ó-gʰē]   Time, moment or period.

Ogechi *nom phr* [ó-gʰ ē-chí], (*var:*
Ogechukwu [ó-gʰ ē-chú-kwú]) God's time or
timing [is the best]. Igbo philosophical thought
is governed by the belief in the fullness of time.
Nothing ever happens before or after the time
God has ordained it to take place. As a result,
when a couple has their child, boy or girl, is the
time appointed by God and nothing can
possibly alter it. Paradoxically, however, the
Igbo also espouse hard work and industry, for
"Onye kwe, Chi ya ekwe" (when a man says
yes, his God says yes also). In other words, you
cannot fold your arms and expect riches to fall
from the sky. These two beliefs are not
contradictory, but complementary; which
means that there are certain things in life

which must be done by man, who will be foolhardy to expect them to be done by God. God will not prosper an indolent person. He prospers the works of your hand. Other life-and-death issues, like childbearing, are God's prerogative and take place at God's appointed time. *Ogechi* is thus an expression of gratitude to God for blessing the couple with a child at His appointed time.

Ojiakọ *nom phr* [ò-jì-à-kó] A shrewd person of ingenious intellect.

Ojinma *nom phr* [ò-jì-n-má]   Beautiful to behold. *Ojinma* literally means 'she who possesses beauty.' This name is normally given to an extremely beautiful baby girl.

Ọlụchi *nom phr* [ó-lú-chī], (*var*: **Ọlụchukwu** [ó-lú-chú-kwú])   God's (handiwork. In addition to the sacredness and sanctity of life, the Igbo hold humans to be God's masterpiece. God – **Chineke** [God the creator] – is a divine "craftsman" whose handiwork is sublime, perfect and without defect. Any defect, therefore, is of human origin, and is believed to be a retribution for an evil deed or unatoned offense against humanity or deity.

Ọlụebube *nom phr* [ó-lú-è-bù-bè], (*var:* Ọrụebube [ó-rú-è-bù-bè]) Miracle.

Ọnụbụọgụ *ut* [ọ-nụ-bụ-ò-gʰ ù] A fight or war normally starts from words of mouth. The power of words in a language in which each syllable is enunciated is clearly conveyed by this name. Words, and by implication, the tone of voice as implied in this name, have the potential to spark off a quarrel, a fight, and indeed, a war. This name is often given in a family or clan where disputes and fights are common as a warning to the 'warring' factions as well as a call to civility and cessation of hostilities.

Onyeọma *nom phr* [ó-nyé-ó-má] A good person.

Onyinyechi *nom phr* [ò-nyì-nyé-chī] A gift from God.

Oriakụ *nom phr* [ò-rí-à-kù] A child who enjoys wealth.

Orienma *nom phr* [ó-rī-è-n-má] Feminine beauty associated with the *Orie* market day. See *Ekenma* for an equivalent name. The only difference is that the girl or woman who bears this name was born on an **Orie** market day.

Osisiọma *nom phr* [ó-sí-sí-ó-má] A lovely tree. See the entry for this name in the Boys' Names section.

Ọsọdiuru *nom phr* [ó-só-dī-ú-rū] A profitable race, meaning a worthy cause. See the entry for this name in the Boys' Names section.

Ọyịm *n* [ò-yím] My friend or my love. Like *Enyioma*, this is one of the affectionate names the Igbo use to communicate love for one another.

S / T

Sọpụrụchi *imp ut* [só-pū-rú-chī], (*var:*
Sọpụrụchukwu [só-pū-rú-chú-kwú])
Have reverence for God.

Tobechi *imp ut* [tò-bé-chī], (*var:*
Tobechukwu [tò-bé-chú-kwú] Praise God.

Toochi *imp ut* [tò-ó-chī], (*var:* **Toochukwu**
[tò-ó-chú-kwú]   Praise God.

U / Ụ

Ụbọchi *n* [ú-bō-chī]   Day.

Uche *n* [ú-chē]   Thought. Opinion. Will.
Judgment. Verdict. This polysemic word refers
to the complex process by which decisions and

worldviews are reached. It is often suffixed by other words for referential precision as in the next three entries.

Uchechi *nom phr* [ú-chē-é-chī] (*var:* **Uchechukwu** [ú-chē-chú-kwú]) God's will.

Uchendu *nom phr* [ú-chē-n-d̂ū] The will to live or the thought of life.

Uchenna *nom phr* [ú-chē-n-nā] Father's will, judgment or verdict.

Ude *n* [ù-dé] Ointment, cream, lotion, oil or fragrance.

Udechukwu *nom phr* [ù-dé-chū-kwū] God's fragrance.

Udenze *nom phr* [ù-dé-n-zē] Chief's ointment or fragrance.

Udeze *nom phr* [ù-dé-zē]   King's fragrance.

Udochi *nom phr* [ù-ɗó-chī] (also: **Udochukwu** [ù-ɗó-chū-kwū])   God's peace.

Udoka *ut* [ù-ɗó-kā]   Peace is [of] supreme [importance.] This name espouses the supremacy of peace in family, societal and communal cohesion. *Udoka* underlines the reason for and importance of striving for peace in interpersonal affairs and relationships.

Ụdụnma *nom phr* [ú-ɗū-n-mà]   Wave-making beauty.

Ụdụnna *nom phr* [ú-ɗū-n-nā]   Father's fame.

Ụfọakụ *nom phr* [ù-fó-ā-kū]   The remnant of wealth.

Ugo *n* [ù-gʰò]   Glory and honour. *Ugo* literally means eagle, the king of birds which is emblematic of power and glory.

Ugoala *nom phr* [ù-gʰó-à-là]   The glory and honour of the land.

Ugochi *nom phr* [ù-gʰó-chī], (*var*: **Ugochukwu** [ù-gʰò-chú-kwú])   God's glory and honour.

Ugochinyere *nom phr* [ù-gʰò-chí-nyē-rē] Honour and glory bestowed by God.

Ugoeze *nom phr* [ù-gʰò-é-zē]   The king's glory and honour.

Ugonna *nom phr* [ù-gʰò-n-nā]   Father's glory and honour.

Ụkaọma *nom phr* [ú-kā-ó-má], (*var*: **Ụkọma** [ú-kō-má])   Good word or conversation; also good report.

Ụkauzọ *nom phr* [ú-kā-ú-zō] Discussion on the road or journey.

Ụkariakụ *ut* [ú-kā-rí-à-kù] A dispute is complicated and expensive.

Ụlọakụ *nom phr* [ú-lō-à-kù] Home or family of riches or wealth. Literally, this name also means a bank. A family did not have to be rich to name their daughter *Ụlọakụ* as this name could be aspirational.

Ụlọma *nom phr* [ú-lō-ó-má] Good home or family (*literally* good house).

Uruchi *nom phr* [ú-rū-chí] Benefits from God.

Ụwaọma *nom phr* [ù-wà-ó-má] Good luck or good fortune.

Ụzọ (*var:* Uzo(h)(r) *n* [ú-zō] The road, understand journey.

Ụzọamaka *ut* [ú-zō-à-má-ká]   The road, or way (or journey) is most beautiful.

Ụzọanya *nom phr* [ú-zō-á-nyā]   A long distance journey.

Ụzọchi *nom phr* [ú-zō-chī], (*var*: Ụzọchukwu [ú-zō-chú-kwú]) God's or godly ways or means.

Ụzọdịnma *nom phr* [ú-zō-dí-n-mā]   A good road or journey. This is basically the same name as *Ụzọma* below. See the entry for *Ijeọma* in this section for names involving a journey.

Ụzọgọ or Uzogo(r) *nom phr* [ú-zō-ó-gō] The road or journey to the family-in-law.

Ụzọha *nom phr* [ú-zō-ò-hà]   The road or way taken by all.

Ụzọhọ *nom phr* [ú-zō-ó-hó-ō] (*var*: Ụzọhụrụ [ú-zō-ó-hú-rū])   A new way or road.

Ụzọije *nom phr* [ú-zō-í-jē] Journey or mission.

Ụzọma *nom phr* [ú-zō-ó-má] A good journey. Just like *Ijeọma*, *Ụzọma* is given as a positive assessment of a successful marriage. Everything said about *Ijeọma* equally applies to *Ụzọma*.

Ụzọndu *nom phr* [ú-zō-n-dʼū] The way of life, also the way to life.

Ụzụnma *nom phr* [ù-zù-n-mā] Wave-making beauty. This is a variant of *Ụdụnma* above.

BIBLIOGRAPHY

Afigbo, Adiele. "Igbo Experience: A Prolegomenon"
in Toyin Falola ed. *Igbo History and Society*:
The Essays of Adiele Afigbo. (Trenton, New Jersey:
African World Press, Inc., 2005), 185-207.

Agbesiere, Joseph Thérèse. *Women in Igbo Life and
Thought*. Dublin: The Holy Rosary Order, 2000.

Agwu, Christopher Agwu. *A Philosophical Concept of
Agwu in Igboland: A Case Study of Ohaozara in
Ebonyi State*. Bloomington, Indiana: Trafford
Publishing, 2013.

Armstrong, R. G. *The Study of West African Languages*. Ibadan: University of Ibadan Press, 1964.

_____ "Glotto-Chronology of West African Linguis-
tics," *Journal of African History* Vol. 3, No. 2
(1962).

Chukukere, Gloria. "Analysis of Cultural Reflection
in Igbo Proverbs" in Rems Nna Umeasiegbu ed.,
13-20.

Echeruo, Michael J. C. *Igbo-English Dictionary:
A Comprehensive Dictionary of the Igbo
Language*. New Haven: Yale University Press,
1998.

Emenanjo, E. Nolue. *Elements of Modern Igbo Grammar*. Ibadan: Oxford University Press, 1978.

Emenyonu, Ernest N. "Preserving the Igbo Language for the 21st Century" in Rems Nna Umeasiegbu, ed. *The Study of Igbo Culture: Essays in Honour of F.C. Ogbalu*. (Enugu: Koruna Books, 1988), 51-63.

Falola, Toyin, ed. *Igbo History and Society: The Essays of Adiele Afigbo*. Trenton, New Jersey: African World Press, Inc., 2005.

Gordon, April A. *Nigeria's Diverse Peoples: A Reference Sourcebook*. Santa Barbara, California: ABC-CLIO, Inc., 2003.

Isichei, Elizabeth. *A History of Christianity in Africa: From Antiquity to the Present*. Lawrenceville, New Jersey: Africa World Press, Inc., 1995.

Ndiokwere, N. I. *Search for Greener Pastures: Igbo And African Experience*. Nebraska: Morris Publishing, 1998.

Ndukaihe, Vernantius Emeka. *Achievement as Value in the Igbo / African Identity: The Ethics*. Berlin: Lit Verlag, 2006.

Njoku, Raphael Chijioke, "Imperial History and the Challenges of Igbo Historical Studies" in Toyin Falola, ed. *Igbo History and Society: the Essays of*

Adiele Afigbo. (Trenton, NJ: 2005), 43-53.

Onuoha, Enyeribe, "The African Traditional World View", Rems Nna Umeasiegbu, ed. *The study of Igbo Culture: Essays in Honour of F.C. Ogbalu.* (Enugu: Koruna Books, 1988), 79–93.

Oraka, L. Nnamdi, "The role of F. C. Ogbalu and the Society for Promoting Igbo Language and Culture in the Promotion of Igbo Education in Nigeria", Rems Nna Umeasiegbu, ed. *The study of Igbo Culture: Essays in Honour or F. C. Ogbalu.* (Enugu: Koruna Books, 1988), 94–106.

Smith, R. S. *Kingdoms of the Yoruba.* Great Britain, 1969.

Uchendu, Victor C. *The Igbo of Southeast Nigeria.* New York: Holt Reinhart and Winston, 1965.

Umeasiegbu, Rems Nna ed. *The Study of Igbo Culture: Essays in Honour of F. C. Ogbalu.* Enugu: Koruna Books, 1988.

Wrigley, C. "Linguistic Clues to African History," *Journal of African History* Vol. 3, No. 2 (1962).

URLs:

https://en.wikipedia.org/wiki/Akanu_Ibiam (Retrieved July 20, 2018).

https://www.researchgate.net/figure/Map-of-Africa-showing-the-location-of-Nigeria-and-Igboland_fig1_27353122 (Retrieved June 02, 2018).

https://www.researchgate.net/figure/Map-of-Igboland-in-Nigeria-Source_fig1_235720609 (Retrieved June 02, 2018).

INDEX

ABOUT THE AUTHOR

Chibuzo N A Uruakpa teaches French in the Languages department of Ethical Culture Fieldston School, New York. Prior to ECFS, he was an Assistant Professor of French at the Defense Language Institute in Monterey, California, and has also taught at Oakwood Friends School, Poughkeepsie, New York, Brooklyn College and Lehman College of The City University of New York, and at the University of Delaware, Newark, Delaware. He holds a doctorate degree in French and Francophone Literature from the Graduate Center, The City University of New York and has master's degrees in French Stylistics and in Bilingual Translation and Interpretation. His research focus is on Francophone African Literature and Culture (Sub-Saharan Africa and the Caribbean), Nineteenth and Twentieth Centuries French Literature, and Bilingual Translation (English-French).

Dr. Uruakpa lives in Westchester, New York, with his wife Vivienne and two daughters.

Printed in Great Britain
by Amazon